BACK STORIES

Further adventures in

COLONEL UNTHANK'S NORWICH

CLIVE LLOYD

BACK STORIES
Further adventures in
Colonel Unthank's Norwich

Clive Lloyd

Published in the United Kingdom by Clive Lloyd

colonelunthanksnorwich.com

Copyright ©Clive Lloyd 2022
ISBN: 978-1-3999-3778-8

The author has made every reasonable effort to provide
correct historical data and to contact copyright holders
of photographs. Please contact:
colonelunthanksnorwich.com for any inadvertent errors
or omissions to be corrected in subsequent printings.
Unless otherwise stated, photographs are by the author.

First printed 2022

Designed by Karen Roseberry

PREFACE

Once again I feel the need to explain a title including the words 'Colonel Unthank's Norwich'. I grew up in an age when songs could be called, 'I was Kaiser Bill's Batman' or 'Sergeant Pepper's Lonely Hearts Club Band', except the reference to Colonel Unthank was not inspired by sixties whimsy but by the monthly blog about historical Norwich that I began in 2015: colonelunthanksnorwich.com. The first short book to emerge from the blog, 'Colonel Unthank and the Golden Triangle', was based on research into the Unthank family, three of whom became colonels in the militia or the regular army. Not only was I fascinated by the unusual name that gave rise to the famous (well, maybe in NR2) Unthank Road, but also with the invasion of Victorian terraces onto the former Unthank estate just beyond the Norwich city walls. Since then I have written about a variety of temporary obsessions.

Writing a post for the scrolling screen is quite a different experience from writing a chapter in a book – PhD theses have been written on the topic – and I've had to rewrite the blog posts to make them suit the static page. Turning a paper page takes you closer, visibly closer, to the end of the book but a continuous stream of words down a screen can sometimes seem endless ('through caverns measureless to man') and the hesitant reader, with no end in sight, has to be enticed over the notional 'fold' at the bottom of the screen. Larding the online text with lots of images helps but having too many in a book can break the flow; I have therefore trimmed some while retaining enough to recapture the richly illustrated feel of the blog.

Apart from roaming around Norwich taking photographs, most of my time preparing a monthly blog post was spent in research. After a lifetime in science I found that visits to the Norfolk Heritage Centre in Norwich Millennium Library, and to the Norfolk Record Office, rekindled the delight of chasing an idea and sometimes finding the unexpected. These small excitements included the discovery that one of the roundels decorating the City Hall doors was originally intended to depict tubes being filled with Norwich's own toothpaste; and that the site of Sir Thomas Browne's garden house is now occupied by Primark; and that instead of installing a classical figure at the top of Commercial Chambers in Red Lion Street – as depicted in a drawing submitted to the Royal Academy – the architect George Skipper inserted a bust of himself with an extravagant moustache more extravagant than Kaiser Bill's.

This book continues on from my second – Colonel Unthank's Norwich: A Sideways Look at the City – based on an eclectic mix of historical topics explored out of curiosity. The chapters in the present book are arranged chronologically but this is not the order in which they were conceived for this collection is just as various as the last: from Norfolk rood screens to the exploits of the sapient pig. You could choose, instead, to treat the contents list as a Chinese buffet that you can dip into randomly rather than a French menu to be ploughed through, from soup to nuts.

Clive Lloyd
November 2022
colonelunthanksnorwich.com
Twitter: @ReggieUnthank

The last thatched houses in Norwich.
Clockwise from top left. In Lion & Castle Yard, Timberhill; The Barking Dicky, Westlegate; The Hampshire Hog, off St Benedict's Street, The Hermitage, Bishopgate; Briton's Arms, Elm Hill; Pykerell's House, St Mary's Plain.

CONTENTS

In 1851, the Gothic Revivalist, Augustus Welby Northmore Pugin, observed that more rood screens were preserved in Norfolk's churches than in any other county. One estimate puts the figure at 275, of which nearly 100 are painted. Some, like the beautiful screen paintings at Barton Turf, are treasures of national importance. This glimpse into pre-Reformation art suggests that a group of artists, probably based in Norwich, may have worked in other media and been receptive to influences from their continental neighbours.

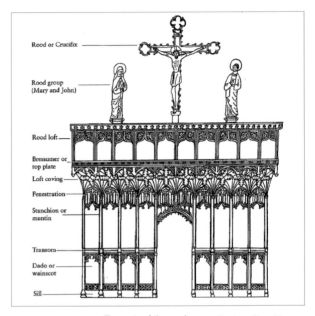

The parts of the rood screen. Courtesy of Lucy Wrapson

Rood screen, St Michael and All Angels, Barton Turf

Although there are earlier examples, the large, carved wooden screens (rarely stone) that we see across the chancel arch today were built around the mid-fifteenth century. These partitions would have been topped by a rood (Saxon for cross), with a crucified Christ flanked by the Virgin Mary and St John the Evangelist.

The upper parts of this complex and by no means standardised superstructure were to disappear during the Tudor Reformation and in the Commonwealth purges that followed. Despite its erratic history (limewashed, put up for sale, placed in the west end), the screen at the Assumption of the Blessed Virgin Mary, Attleborough, is now restored to its rightful place at the east end and provides a sense of what used to be.

From wall to wall the screen is 52 feet wide and in terms of size and completeness is unmatched in East Anglia. Above and behind the rare rood loft are painted figures in the tympanum once covered by whitewash. Like many of its counterparts throughout the country this screen is in Perpendicular style – the style that dominated church building from the latter part of the fourteenth century until the Reformation of the sixteenth century, when the evolution of ecclesiastical architecture stalled.

Neighbouring Suffolk has a more complete tympanum painting at St Peter, Wenhaston (not shown). In 1892 this wooden structure was taken down and, famously, left out in the rain, revealing the painting beneath the whitewash. This 'doom' painting illustrates the Day of Doom or Judgement Day when God decides which soul goes to heaven and which to hell. Norfolk has its own accidentally discovered tympanum at Ludham

The rood screen at Attleborough

St Catherine, which had lain in the unused rood stair until it was discovered in 1879 during an Archaeological Society outing. To the side of the reduced screen, at bottom and top, there are orphaned doorways (arrowed) that once gave access to the rood loft but now lead nowhere. It is possible that the rediscovered painting may have been hastily installed during the brief reign of the Catholic Mary Tudor who worked to reverse the iconoclasm begun during the reign of her father, Henry VIII.

When she came to the throne, Elizabeth I countermanded the changes begun by her half-sister. Elizabeth's Royal Order of 1561 directed that the rood figures in the loft should be taken down but 'a comely partition between the chancel and the church' should remain (or a new one erected), topped with a suitable crest or the Royal Arms. Elizabeth's arms can be seen on the reverse of the Ludham tympanum, although they now face the altar. The royal edict to retain a partition would explain why England has so many screens. And Norfolk may have kept so many painted dado screens because, during the Civil War, 'Smasher' Dowsing focused more on Suffolk and Cambridgeshire.

The screen had served to insulate the congregation in the nave from the mysteries enacted around the altar

Rood screen. Ludham

– a permeable barrier to remind lay people of the distinction between this life and the life hereafter. But by 1638 the Bishop of Norwich, Richard Montague, was voicing a more worldly view of the function of the screen:

'Is your chancel divided from the nave or body of your church ... is there a decent strong door to open and shut ... with lock and key, to keep out boys, girls or irreverent men and women? and are dogs kept from coming to besoil or profane the Lord's table?'.

None of the rood-screen painters left their name but attempts have been made to group their works stylistically. The mirror to which all other paintings are held is the fifteenth century screen at St Helen's Ranworth in the heart of the Norfolk Broads, probably the best known rood screen in the country. The screen itself contains paintings of the 12 apostles while the

St Michael slaying the seven-headed dragon of the apocalypse; St George and the dragon. Ranworth.

St Barbara overseen by an angel (enlarged)

adjoining parclose screens (above) contain two highly mannered and exceptional paintings of St George and St Michael.

The Ranworth St Michael has been described as debonair or detached but despite his languor he seems to have warmed to his task by separating the dragon from two of its seven heads. These paintings, over twice the width of those on the rood screen, provide greater room for arm-waving than allowed the 12 constricted saints on the rood screen panels. Stylistically, the demi-figures painted above saints in the reredos panels are reminiscent of the elegant feather-suited angels of the fifteenth century Norwich School of Glass Painting whose output can be found throughout the county. (There were three chapters on Norwich School angels in my previous book).

Circled and enlarged in the tracery above St Barbara is a sorrowful angel with the same blond corkscrew locks as St Michael. Along with her martyr's palm leaf, St Barbara holds the tower in which she was kept from the world. Her gown of rich brocade turns out to be significant when building an argument for a school of rood screen painters.

Another comparison with glass painting: in his key book on *The Norwich School of Glass-Painting in the Fifteenth Century*, Christopher Woodforde pointed out that ermine 'tippets' (short shoulder capes), of the kind worn by the demi-figures of angels at Ranworth, were also worn by angels in Norwich School glass. In the next figure, both angels wear tippets with tadpole-like black tails on the ermine (circled), both have tight blond curls and the wing feathers have been handled in a similar way – all pointing to a common inspiration.

L: Demi-figure from the Ranworth rood screen. R: Painted glass angel from St Peter's, Ringland.

St George and the Dragon. L: St Gregory's Norwich. R: by Rogier van der Weyden. National Gallery of Art, Washington.

The 'Ranworth style' as exemplified by the flamboyant saints, George and Michael, is a late and refined version of Northern Italian 'International Gothic', characterised – according to historian John Mitchell – by the 'melodiously flowing' garments that fall away from the body almost independently of the underlying limbs'. It may have taken some time to get here but Norfolk artists would not have been immune to a continental movement for this was a region grown rich from trading with its neighbours across the North Sea. The artist who took over John Wighton's fifteenth century glass-painting workshop in Norwich, John Mundeford, was a Dutchman and it is reasonable to suppose that the city's other artists would have been aware of the transformative effects of Italian Renaissance art filtered through a Northern European sensibility.

The works of the well-known Netherlandish Rogier van der Weyden (ca.1400-1464), for instance, had been in circulation for over half a century before the equestrian painting on the wall of St Gregory's Norwich is believed to have been painted. There are several points of similarity, including the general pose of horse and rider, and the presence of a young woman hovering in the background. And, as noted by Audrey Baker, the alternating lilies and roses in the garland worn by St Cecilia in the rood screen at North Elmham are borrowed from the headdress of the Virgin Mary, from Jan van Eyck's (d 1441) Ghent altarpiece.

A headdress of lilies and roses. L: Jan van Eyck's Ghent altarpiece (public domain). R: St Cecilia, North Elmham.

THE RANWORTH GROUP

Membership of the Ranworth Group has evolved over the years. Originally five, there now appears to be a settled core of seven: Ranworth, North Elmham, Old Hunstanton, Thornham, the apostle paintings at Southwold, Filby, and paintings from St James, Pockthorpe Norwich removed to St Mary Magdalene Norwich. An unfinished panel of St Apollonia from St Augustine's Norwich – now in St Peter Hungate and restored by Lucy Wrapson – could be an eighth. To this eight, Lucy Wrapson adds North Walsham as well as the Great Plumstead panels lost to fire in 1891 and known only from Victorian illustrations. As we will see, common motifs unite the ten rood-screen paintings.

In a magnificent book on East Anglian rood screen painting, based on her thesis of 1937, Audrey Baker observed two details found in the Ranworth Group (with the possible exception of North Walsham). The first was the inclusion of animal or bird motifs in the rich brocades, based on Italian designs, worn by the apostles and virgins; this led to the Ranworth Group being called the 'damask workshop'. Damask is a patterned fabric woven from mixed fibres, sometimes silk, much richer and lighter than the pure-wool worsteds that had been the Norfolk staple before the Norwich Strangers brought their expertise for making the New Draperies.

All Saints, Thornham

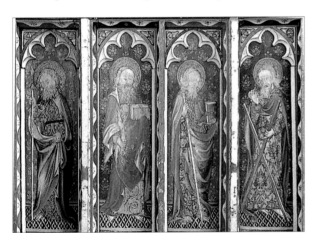

St Helen's, Ranworth

All Saints, Filby

St Andrew's, Old Hunstanton (St Andrew far right)

St Edmund's, Southwold. One of a pair of central Apostles panels. Possibly the last surviving example of the Ranworth Group c1500.

St Mary's North Elmham

Norwich, ex St James Pockthorpe now at St Mary Magdalene. Bought by JJ Colman from a Norwich market, 1880s. Restored and heavily overpainted. Removed to StMM when StJP was converted to Norwich Puppet Theatre in 1982.

Rich brocades and tiled floors at St Helen's, Ranworth.

The figure of St Paul from the Ranworth screen illustrates the richness of brocade; it also shows a second motif identified by Audrey Baker: the 'counterchanged' tiles on which the figures stand. In all seven members of the inner Ranworth Group the saints' feet have been painted against a background of tiles represented as a two-dimensional vertical pattern. Instead of the tiles receding away into the painting, as they would have done in Flemish paintings of the time, their lack of perspective produces the effect of a skirting board. In their flatness, the tiles are usually placed diagonally with a central circular inset in which two colours are reversed.

A third common feature was identified by Baker: a floral pattern in the background, usually stencilled in gold leaf. One such pattern resembles a loosely tied bunch of flowers, another depicts a pomegranate. The figure below shows the botanical stencils along with the geometrical floor tiles shared by the seven core members of the Ranworth Group. The stencilling around the Southwold apostles – probably the last survivors of the Ranworth group to have been painted, around 1500 – is pushed up into the tracery by the gold gesso background and the stencilled botanical patterns at Filby are all but faded. The saints in the North Walsham panels do not stand on chequered floor tiles but they do have botanical stencils in the background, drawing them in closer orbit to the nucleus of seven.

In the larger group recognised by Lucy Wrapson is a ninth set of screen paintings that had been lost when the rood screen at Great Plumstead perished in the fire of

Found on all screens in the core Ranworth Group, geometrical tiles at bottom and floral stencilling above.

The Ranworth Nose. Top: demi-angel, Ranworth (reversed [r] for easier comparison); St Cecilia North Elmham [r]; St Martin Great Plumstead [r]. Bottom: St Cecilia Filby; St John Old Hunstanton; St Helena Pockthorpe (now at St Mary Magdalene Norwich).

1891. Fortunately, artist Cornelius Jansson Walter Winter made copies in 1859 and these can be seen online at the Norfolk Museums Collections. Winter's drawings confirm that the chequered tiles and stencilled background were present in the Great Plumstead rood screen.

If you stare long enough at all these saints and angels a stereotypical facial type emerges and can be glimpsed in some, though by no means all, of the Ranworth Group. Screen figures are often defaced (especially the eyes and mouth) and details may have been dulled or exaggerated during restoration; the Pockthorpe figures, in particular, have been heavily overpainted. Nevertheless, there does seem to be a formula consisting of a mournful face in profile, the head slightly bowed, and a long thin nose that has a defined bulb at the end (retroussé, ski-jump?). It is better shown than described.

The similarities between these and other satellites of the Ranworth Group suggest that a workshop of painters used studio cartoons as is known to be the case for Norfolk stained-glass painters. The use of stock figures is particularly obvious at North Elmham where all the female saints are painted from the same model – some

reversed – and only differentiated by the attributes they carry: e.g., St Barbara with her castle.

A NORWICH SCHOOL OF ARTISTS?
In the fifteenth through to the sixteenth century, Norwich was a regional centre for glass painting. Alderman John Wighton's workshop was preeminent in the latter part of the fifteenth century then around 1500 the practice of Alderman William Heyward came to the fore. There is good evidence that Heyward's workshop produced inscribed monumental brasses as well as painted glass, probably south of the river around what is now the redundant church of St Peter Parmentergate off King Street. When Heyward had been apprenticed to Thomas Goldbeater as a glazier, Richard Steere was apprenticed as a painter, again suggesting that drawing skills were used in more than one medium. From evidence such as this, the authority on late medieval Norwich glass, David King, has argued that Heyward ran a multi-media workshop that may also have been involved in painting rood screens and walls – perhaps even the mural of St George and the Dragon in St Gregory's Norwich.

Dorothy Parker's wisecrack, that members of the Bloomsbury Group lived in squares, painted in circles and loved in triangles, couldn't possibly apply to Norwich. We have circles and, one suspects, triangles, but we just don't have squares; instead we have plains. A tour of the city's plains gives us the lie of the land.

Plains aren't restricted to Norwich for you'll stumble across them across Norfolk and Suffolk. The word for an open space seems to be an import from the Low Countries as I saw pre-Covid when visiting friends near Reddingsplein in Amsterdam.

In 1566 the Fourth Duke of Norfolk requested Queen Elizabeth's permission to invite 'thirty Douchemen' to help revive Norwich's flagging textile trade. The following year this trickle became a flood when Protestants from the Spanish Netherlands fled the murderous intolerance of Philip II of Spain. The word 'plain', however, predated these arrivals: Nicholas Sotherton's eye-witness account of Kett's 1549 rebellion refers to 'the playne before the pallace gate' so the word was an earlier introduction, part of the city's already long association with the Low Countries.

St Martin at Palace Plain – now the site of John Sell Cotman's house – was where, in 1549, a pitched battle was fought between the king's forces and Robert Kett's rebels (but remember, one man's rebel is another man's freedom fighter). Here, Lord Sheffield fell from his horse and, as was the custom, he removed his helmet expecting to be ransomed. But the butcher Fulke, unschooled in the rules of chivalry, bludgeoned Sheffield to death. The duke and 35 others were buried in the adjacent church, St Martin at Palace.

St Paul's Plain no longer exists. The octagonal top of the tower, rebuilt with white bricks around 1819, survived the incendiary bombs of 1942. Had it been been preserved – just as St Benedict's tower was left to stand alone – it would be the largest of the city's five

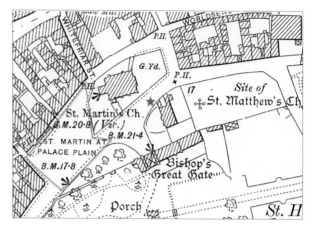

St Martin at Palace Plain. Blue star, where Lord Sheffield was killed.
© Ordnance Survey 1905.

St Paul's church 1937. ©georgeplunkett.co.uk

round towers. But according to the City Engineer's 1944 Plan for Norwich it stood in the way of post-war improvement and the site was cleared in preparation for the St Crispin's Road flyover and the Barrack Street roundabout. The church was founded in the twelfth century as a hospital for poor strangers. It was also recorded in the sixteenth century being used as a bridewell (prison) before William Appleyard's house took over that function in what is now Bridewell Alley.

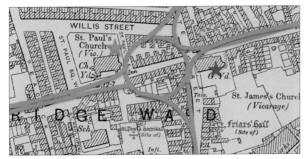

1970 flyover (left) and Barrack St roundabout superimposed on 1884 OS map. Red star, St Paul's church. Blue star, St James' church/Norwich Puppet Theatre.

The site is now a small public garden and children's play area. The evidence, though, for calling the space 'St Paul's Plain' is slim. *White's Directory* of 1845 describes it as 'the square called St Paul's plain' and – surrounded by streets on four sides – it does look on Samuel King's map of 1766 more like a square, albeit somewhat on the

huh (East Anglian for wonky). 'Square' may work in this instance but, as we will see, is a poor definition of the other variously irregular open spaces. The explanation provided by local author George Nobbs' comes closer: 'In Norwich the term Plain is usually used to describe the area of a meeting of streets'.

Agricultural Hall Plain. At one time the castle was ringed by various livestock markets for which the Agricultural Hall of 1882 provided formal focus. The sloping plain outside the Hall stands at the top of Prince of Wales Road, a wide, curving street built in 1865 to connect Norwich Thorpe Railway Station to the city's commercial heart. The street was never finished as planned and is only graceful in parts although Pevsner and Wilson thought the buildings on the plain at the top of the road 'dignify the new entry to the city'. The photograph below shows: Barclays Bank's huge banking hall, designed by the local firm of E Boardman

Agricultural Hall Plain

Harvey's Crown Bank

is seen as a legacy of the postal service that left the building in 1970, but it is, in reality, a distant memory of Major Money's service in upstate New York.

Before we leave Agricultural Hall Plain we should take some cheer from knowing that Laurel and Hardy stayed in the Royal Hotel in 1954.

Bank Plain is the conjoined twin of Agricultural Hall Plain, connected by the former Barclays Bank that runs between the two. Built as late as 1929 in a style reminiscent of an Italian palazzo, Barclays stands on the site of Gurneys, Birkbeck, Barclays and Buxton Bank, established by Quakers in the late eighteenth century. Originally, this open space was called Redwell Plain but, after Gurney's opened, it became known as Bank Plain. The plain might be imagined to be limited to the flaring out of London Street where it ends at Redwell Street but the 1884 OS map shows this running all the way up to Agricultural Hall Plain.

& Son with Brierley & Rutherford of York (1929); the statue of Peace sculpted by George and Fairfax Wade (1904), a monument to the Boer War; the Royal Hotel, another local masterwork by the Boardmans (1896-7) and decorated in red brick from Gunton's Costessey Brickworks; then there is the Agricultural Hall itself, built in alien red Cumberland sandstone relieved with decorative Cosseyware.

The Agricultural Hall was inaugurated in 1882 by the Patron of the Norwich Fat Cattle Show Association – the Prince of Wales, the future King Edward VII. In the same year Oscar Wilde started his lecture tour of America. Two years later he visited the Agricultural Hall to deliver his lecture on 'The House Beautiful' to the possibly bemused cattlemen of the Norfolk plains.

An earlier resident of this plain, Crown Bank (1866), was built by Sir Robert Harvey and named after his Crown Point estate, just outside the city at Whitlingham. Harvey had bought the estate from Major Money, who was not a banker but an intrepid balloonist and soldier who had served at Fort Crown Point in North America. Harvey shot himself after his dubious investments discredited the bank. Later, when the Post Office occupied the building, the crown sculpted on the parapet was easily repurposed by adding the words, 'Post Office'. Fifty years on, history blurs and the crown

Gurney's, Birkbeck, Barclay and Buxton Bank on Bank Plain. Rebuilt in the 1920s as Barclays. © Barclays Group Archives

Today, it is possible to travel to nearby **St Andrew's (Hall) Plain** by following the bend in the road down the hill to Suckling House aka Cinema City. The 1884 OS map shows that this extension of St Andrew's Street

The bisected Garsett/Armada House

than the tortuous medieval alleyways, that pitched battles could be fought. Sotherton saw Kett's bowmen let loose 'a mighty force of arrowes'... 'as flakes of snow in a tempest' but Captain Drury's band of arquebusiers, with their early versions of the musket, replied with 'such a terrible volley of shot (as if there had been a storm of hayle)', leaving about 330 dead.

St Andrew's Hall Plain 1896.
Courtesy of Norfolk County Council Library and Information Service

did not exist at that time; it was created so that the new electric trams, which arrived with the twentieth century, could avoid the tight corner where Redwell Street meets Princes Street. To help the new tramway negotiate the bend, houses were demolished and Garsett House was bisected. This timber-framed house of 1589 is said to have been built from the timbers of a ship wrecked during the Spanish Armada and bears the alternative name of Armada House.

St Andrew's Hall is the nave of what was the Blackfriars or Dominican church of Norwich – the most complete surviving medieval friary in England. Blackfriars Hall was originally the friars' chancel and after the Dissolution it became the church of the Dutch-speaking community. The large internal volume of St Andrew's Hall was designed by the Dominicans for spreading the word just as the plain outside was used as a preaching yard. During Kett's Rebellion this open space witnessed less peaceable activity for it was on the plains, rather

The legitimacy of **St George's Plain** as a plain is beyond question for it is enshrined in Pevsner and Wilson's *Buildings of England*. It is a part of Colegate, on which the Tudor and Georgian houses of rich wool merchants still stand. On the 1886 OS map the plain appears as a widening of the road between a block labelled 'Boot and Shoe Manufactory' and the churchyard of St George's Colegate (ca.1459). St George's – a fine church with austere Georgian furnishings – was one of the few things in the city that the architectural commentator Ian Nairn could persuade himself to like. John Crome, co-founder of the Norwich Society of Artists, lived around the corner and is buried here.

Howlett and White's factory, with its two-hundred foot facade by Boardman, was once the country's

Howlett & White's shoe factory opposite St George's Colegate

Anglo-Scandinavian period, a defended trading settlement, or wic, on the north bank of the river minted its own coins stamped with the word Norvic. Colegate is part of that north wic.

For centuries, the clack of hand looms could be heard from the attic rooms of numerous houses, especially in Norwich-over-the-Water. Weaving wool and silk was the basis of the city's fame and wealth but the industry was always fragmented and workers staunchly resisted the move into factories, unlike the mills of northern England and Scotland that had better access to fast-running water or coal to run their large power looms. At the beginning of the nineteenth century, Norwich's trade in textiles was in terminal decline and by the end of the century factory-based shoe-making had taken over as our major industry. These two trades are represented by the saw-tooth roofline of the Norvic-Kiltie shoe factory (across the road from Howlett & White's main factory) and the pub that was known in the eighteenth century as the Crown & Woolpack then The Woolpacket and, more recently, The Gatherers.

largest producer of footwear under one roof. The tower on the Colegate facade separates the two phases of major expansion. In 1909 the company introduced the brand name Norvic and in 1935 the business itself was renamed the Norvic Shoe Company Ltd. Norvic, short for Norvicensis, is the salutation adopted by the Bishop of Norwich but it can be traced back to a time before the Normans raised their great cathedral. In the preceding

Leather vs wool: the Norvic-Kiltie shoe factory and a pub dedicated to the weaving industry

Maddermarket Plain is one of the city's smaller plains. It is situated at the junction of St Andrew's Street, Duke Street, St John Maddermarket (formerly St John's Street) and Charing Cross. The names of the latter two streets provide a clue to the history of this district. 'Madder', of course, refers to the red/deep pink dye derived from madder roots, used to colour fabric the famous Norwich Red. And 'Charing Cross' is believed to be a corruption of 'shearing' – the process by which the raised pile on woollen cloth was trimmed to a uniform height.

Maddermarket Plain (rectangular box). Blue line, churchyard wall demolished for Queen Elizabeth's procession. © Ordnance Survey.

The Charing Cross/Westwick Street area was at the heart of the textile industry and the river was where its waste products ended up. In early maps, Fuller's Lane appears within the Charing Cross district – fulling being the process by which cloth was cleaned. In the nineteenth century, from his factory on the opposite bank to the duke's palace, the master dyer Michael Stark emptied his vats into the Wensum. This kind of pollution had been happening for centuries for, on his journeys

through England in 1681, Thomas Baskerville noted that the duke's great townhouse was 'seated in a dung-hole place', surrounded by tradesmen cleaning and dyeing cloth. The palace was later abandoned.

When Queen Elizabeth I visited Norwich in 1578 she was greeted inside St Stephen's Gate by tableaux depicting the city's trades, including young girls demonstrating the skills of her 'Douchemen' weavers. Afterwards, the queen had to be conveyed by carriage from the Guildhall on Market Hill down to the duke's palace, a short journey but, to the medieval coach driver negotiating medieval streets, the equivalent of threading a needle. During the reign of William IV (1832) the solution was to connect the Duke's Palace

Graveyard wall of St John Maddermarket

with the marketplace by demolishing houses to make way for Exchange Street: the Elizabethan solution was to widen the street of St John Maddermarket (now St John's Street) by shaving some of the eastern side of the church's overpopulated graveyard and rebuilding the six-foot high wall (see the blue line on the map opposite).

The 1884 Ordnance Survey map appears to show **St Margarets Plain** occupying much the same space as it does today, although local author Richard Lane noted that Westwick Street 'used to widen slightly at this point until pre-war demolition and German bombs altered the northern side completely.'

St Margaret in the spandrel of her church.

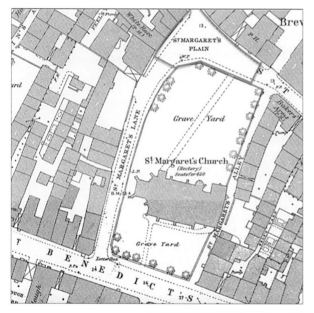

St Margaret's Plain. © Ordnance Survey 1884

St Margaret is purported to be the figure carved in the left hand spandrel above the church porch. In his book on *Norwich Plains*, Richard Lane generally found *White's Directory* of 1845 to be a useful source of addresses as supplied by trade subscribers themselves yet he could find no mention of **St Benedict's Plain**. He did mention

an unnamed author who located the plain to the place where Pottergate, Willow Lane, Cow Hill and Ten Bell Lane met; 'others' defined it as the widening of Pottergate from Ten Bell Lane westwards, nearer to the church itself. The body of the church was a victim of the war but the flint tower itself stands as a reproach to those who believed the tower of St Paul's, over the water, not worth saving. Although St Benedict's Plain was not on the 1884 or 1904 OS maps I did manage to confirm its existence on several modern records, including The National Archives' website, which revealed that the Norfolk and Norwich Eye Infirmary stood on St Benedict's Plain from 1823-1854.

Clearly, our plains were provisional spaces with uncertain boundaries, difficult to capture by locals and map-makers alike. We will read about the remaining Plains after a diversion around the Paston family in Norwich.

We know much about the rise of Norfolk's Paston family from the cache of letters left in the eighteenth century by the last of the line, William Paston, 2nd Duke of Yarmouth. It was from the duke's estate that local antiquarian Francis Blomefield acquired part of the Paston Letters. This correspondence gives unique insight into one family's life (1422 to 1509), illustrating how – in the long period following the halving of the population by the Black Death – the descendants of a feudal serf would become elevated to the aristocracy. But it was probably the weakness of this foundation that led to the later Pastons being assailed by the Dukes of Norfolk and Suffolk who disputed their title to land.

The story starts with Clement Paston (d1419), from the village of Paston about 20 miles north-east of Norwich. He was 'a good, plain husband' whose lowly station in life was illustrated by the fact that he had to ride, 'to mill on the bare horseback with his corn under him'. Clement was probably a bondman not entitled under feudal law to own land and these humble origins were to be used against his descendants as they rose to prominence. The rise began when, with the assistance of his brother-in-law, Clement was able to pay for a grammar school education for his son William who then studied law in London and eventually became a Judge of Common Pleas. In addition to purchasing land in the village of

Paston, William bought his favourite manor Oxnead in 1419 and Gresham Castle in 1427. Eventually, the descendants of a man troubled by transporting his own corn would be able to build one of the largest barns in the county – the 70 metre-long barn in the village of Paston.

William married Agnes Barry and they had four sons and a daughter. The first was John Paston I (1421-1466), another lawyer, who married the redoubtable Margaret Mautby. They named two of their sons John: John II (1442-1479) and John III (1444-1504), not just to flummox future historians but probably in honour of Margaret's father, John or possibly of a relative of hers who would play an unwitting part in the Pastons' troubled history – Sir John Fastolf.

Although much of the story revealed in the Paston Letters was set in the county, the Pastons had a significant presence in the city of Norwich. A green plaque announces that a John Paston lived in a house on King Street after 1478. This was in what is now the oldest dwelling house in the city, Jurnet's House, named after the Jewish trader who arrived here in the twelfth

The Paston Barn, Paston, Norfolk

Jurnet's House, King Street, Norwich

Paston House (Strangers Club), Elm Hill

– the beam crisply carved with Steward's personal insignia at one end and, in recognition of his trade, the mark of the Mercers' Company at the other.

The wealthy cloth merchant also owned Steward's House, the leaning building over the entrance to Tombland Alley. Next door is Samson and Hercules House where the eponymous heroes hold up the porch. This building, with four Norwich lucams (dormers), was built in 1656 on the site of a house once owned by the Pastons' relative, Sir John Fastolf (1380-1459). In another of those collisions so frequent in this densely historic city, Fastolf would have been able to look across Tombland to the effigy of another soldier mentioned in Shakespeare, Sir Thomas Erpingham (1357-1428), Henry V's captain of archers at Agincourt. In its niche above the cathedral's Erpingham Gate the knight's statue depicts him kneeling in prayer, an attitude that may have been a deliberate riposte to the claim that he was a Lollard (pre-Reformation objector to practices of the Catholic Church) – a claim also levelled at Fastolf himself.

century. It was rare at the time for being built of stone. Now it is Wensum Lodge Adult Education Centre.

John I and Margaret had a town house on Elm Hill where some of the Paston Letters were probably written. This house was victim to a great fire in 1507 that destroyed half the city. The fire raged for days in Elm Hill, laying waste to all except the three-storey timber-framed building known latterly as Briton's Arms. Much of the street was rebuilt by Sheriff of Norwich and three-times Mayor, Augustine Steward. This included the Pastons' house, occupied today by the Strangers Club. Access to Crown Court Yard around the back is gained beneath a sixteenth century beam across the alleyway

Steward's House and Samson & Hercules House, Tombland

The Mercer's Maiden (l); Steward's personal insignia (r)

The Erpingham family also contributed large sums of money to the lengthy restoration of the Blackfriars' church in nearby St Andrew's Plain, which was damaged by an earlier fire of 1413. Backing onto Elm Hill, what we now know as Blackfriar's Hall was formerly the chancel of the great friary church and the adjoining St Andrew's Hall was the nave. The complex was only sixty or so yards from the Pastons' house and John and Margaret are known to have paid for the restoration of roof beams in Blackfriars and the hammer beams in St Andrews. During the Reformation, Augustine Steward purchased the buildings on behalf of the city, 'to make the church a fayer and large hall'; 'The Halls' are still used as public spaces. As you enter St Andrew's Hall, look for John Paston's and Margaret Mautby's coats of arms on the fifteenth century doors they installed.

St Peter Hungate at top of Elm Hill

The Paston/Mautby arms on door to St Andrew's Hall

A few further steps up Elm Hill is the church of St Peter Hungate at the junction with the street known as Hungate or Princes Street. John and Margaret owned what may have been an overspill property on this street; they also worshipped at the church. Between 1458-60 the Pastons funded the rebuilding of the nave and transepts. High in the south transept are two decorative corbels – one depicting a man's head, the other a woman's – that are thought to commemorate the donors.

This has been an intentionally blinkered look at the Pastons in Norwich but the great dramas surrounding this family were played out in the county, against a broader backdrop of national instability during the Wars of the Roses. The Pastons were to be besieged in three of their houses. First, in 1448 Lord Moleyns laid claim to Gresham Castle, which William Paston had bought from Thomas, the son of poet Geoffrey Chaucer. With the support of the powerful Duke of Suffolk, Moleyns sent 1000 armed men to expel Margaret who famously wrote to her husband in London to send crossbows and poleaxes. In the event, after Moleyns' men mined the walls of Margaret's chamber she was 'plukkyd out of here howse' then her mansion destroyed.

The greatest upturn in the Pastons' fortunes came at the death of their kinsman, the fabulously wealthy soldier Sir John Fastolf, to whom John had become legal adviser. John claimed that two days before the old soldier died (1459) he had made a verbal will agreeing to sell him all his Suffolk and Norfolk lands for the bargain price of 4000 marks provided that John oversaw the foundation of a chantry at Caister to pray for Fastolf's soul. It was perhaps inevitable that disinherited heirs and local noblemen would contest a deathbed will dictated in the presence of the main beneficiary. In 1461, a month after the coronation of the new king (Edward IV), the Duke of Norfolk felt able to take direct action by besieging Caister Castle with 3,000 men. There were further altercations but the castle was not to be returned to John Paston II until after the restoration of Henry VI in 1470.

The Pastons also inherited Fastolf's manors in Hellesdon and Drayton but in 1466 the powerful Duke of Suffolk seized Drayton, just across the Wensum from his own stronghold in Costessey. He then attacked their manor at Hellesdon, not only destroying what had been Margaret's home for the last six years, but ransacking their tenants' houses and even the church. Suffolk evidently felt that as the king's brother-in-law, and with the Mayor of Norwich in his pocket, he could act with impunity.

C15 Plaisance associated with Fastolf and the Pastons. Drayton Lodge.

In 1466 John Paston died in London and over six days his body was conveyed back to Norfolk, accompanied by a priest and twelve torchbearers. The cost of the funeral exceeded £250, more than a year's income from the Paston estates. By surrounding the occasion with such pomp and extravagance the Pastons seemed to be thumbing a nose to the local aristocracy for subjecting the family to years of turbulence. The hearse cost more than £30; cloth for the mourners, £20; alms and doles to be distributed to the poor, more than £60. John Paston's body rested for one night at St Peter Hungate before completing the journey to Bromholm Priory, near Bacton, where his father had been buried.

Bromholm Priory near Bacton had become a major site of medieval pilgrimage after a large piece of the true cross was brought from Constantinople and incorporated into the priory's Holy Rood. Twenty-two pounds worth of candles illuminated the hearse and such was the stench of burning tallow that a glazier had to be paid 20 pence to remove two panes of glass 'to late out the reke of the torches'. The mourners at John Paston's funeral feasted on 49 pigs, 49 calves, 10 cows, 34 lambs and 22 sheep that had taken two men more than three days to flay.

Bromholm Priory gatehouse

Margaret Paston died in 1484 and is buried in her home church of Mautby, not far from Caister. St Peter and St Paul, Mautby. Following the demolition of an aisle during the Reformation, Margaret Paston's grave is now on the outside of the south wall.

Saints Peter and Paul, Mautby

The descendants of Margaret and John lived in less turbulent times. William Paston, 1st Baronet founded North Walsham School; his son Robert, First Earl of Yarmouth, was a Fellow of the Royal Society who corresponded with Sir Thomas Browne about his experiments to transmute base metals into gold; his son William, the Second Earl of Yarmouth, was Member of Parliament and, like his father, FRS.

When the Second Earl died in 1732 his titles died with him. Amongst his possessions was the Paston Treasure, a painting of the Paston collections once held at Oxnead Hall. Painted around the middle of the seventeenth century, in the manner of Dutch vanity paintings, it depicts some of the objects amassed by his father and grandfather, both of whom had travelled through Europe to the Middle East. As a founding member of the Royal Society his father's collection might be thought to have come from his cabinet of curiosities. However, there are so many symbols of the transience and futility of life (hourglass, watch, guttering candle, lute with broken string, a falling flagon) that it is more a vanitas painting depicting the vanities of a fleeting life, than a depiction of his cabinet of curiosities. The most heart-breaking counterbalance to all of the Paston vanities is the image of a pretty young girl; whether Mary Paston or her older sister Margaret she holds roses in full bloom, a poignant reminder that all things must pass. Do visit the Paston Treasure at Norwich Castle Museum.

The Paston Treasure, Dutch School (ca1650), Norwich Castle Museum and Art Gallery.

London has its famous residential squares, built to enclose green space and exclude the surrounding poverty. These enclaves mainly arose during the Georgian and Victorian periods and from the outset were part of the designed urban landscape. Norwich, on the other hand, has very few formal, rectangular spaces. The Anglo-Scandinavian marketplace, Tombland (meaning empty space), and the Norman marketplace, are both rectangular but neither of these was called a 'plain' for they pre-dated the arrival of the Dutch who gave the name to our open spaces. And although we can point to several isolated Georgian gems there was never sufficient development within the confines of a walled city based on a medieval street plan (if 'plan' is the word) to add up to an eighteenth century square. The nearest thing to a London-like square is the Cathedral Close but although some of its houses are Georgian it is Norman in origin.

Some plains have been so eroded by tramways, motor traffic, World War II and post-war improvement that we may wonder whether they existed at all; **St Catherine's Plain** is one such open space. It was the land surrounding the pre-Conquest church of St Catherine

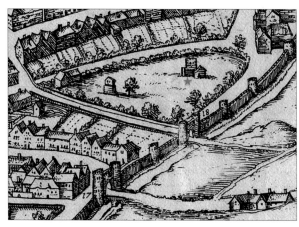

The solitary church in St Catherine's Close. Braun and Hogenberg's map of 1581. Photo: the author. Courtesy of Norfolk County Council

that was given to the nuns at Carrow by King Stephen. Now it is one of Norwich's lost churches and its demise can be traced to the plague that almost depopulated the parish. The historian Blomefield (1705-1752) mentions that the Close consisted of a solitary house, which was already the case in 1581 when Braun and Hogenberg recorded it on their plan of the city.

The Georgian side of Lower Cathedral Close

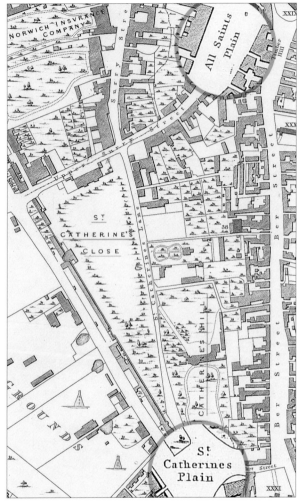

St Catherine's Plain (circled), with Close, Lane and Hill underlined. Millard & Manning's map (1830). Photo: the author. Courtesy of Norfolk County Council

The Thatched Assembly Rooms 1935 © georgeplunkett.co.uk

reminders of the former extent of St Catherine's parish. Millard and Manning's map also identified the nearby **All Saints Plain** outside the present-day John Lewis store, known to older residents as 'Bonds'. Samuel King's map of 1766 calls it by its present-day name of All Saints Green and supplies another alternative of 'Old Swine Market' – a further reminder of the livestock markets that once encircled the castle.

Born 1844 in Ludham, Robert Herne Bond owned a shop in Ber Street and bought adjoining properties that allowed him to extend through to All Saints Plain. Bond had bought a set of thatched cottages from a Major Crowe who had restored them in the late nineteenth century. These, the Thatched Assembly Rooms, were later converted to a ballroom then a cinema. When Bond acquired the buildings he re-converted The Thatched Cinema to a ballroom for his staff; it was also used as a restaurant and furnishing hall. The 'Thatched' was destroyed by incendiary bombs in 1942. Immediately the war ended, Bond's son, the architect J Owen Bond, replaced this collection of rustic-looking vernacular buildings with a modernist department store. In 1982, Bonds of Norwich was taken over by John Lewis.

From All Saints Green it is a short hop down Westlegate to an open space that appears, though unnamed,

A reminder of the plain just outside St Catherine's Close can be found on the east side of modern-day Queen's Road. Between the junction with Finkelgate and the twentieth century junction with Surrey Street is a treed area still marked with an older style cast-iron street sign – 'St Catherines Plain'. Finkelgate itself was once called St. Catherine's Street while Millard and Manning's map of 1830 shows St Catherine's Close, Hill and Lane, all

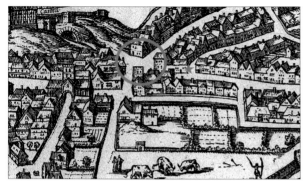

St Stephens Plain (circled) on Braun and Hogenberg's map 1581. Asterisk, The Boar's Head.

on Braun and Hogenberg's map of 1581. This is **St Stephens Plain** formed at the crossroads between Westlegate/Rampant Horse Street bisected by St Stephen's Street/Red Lion Street. From the nineteenth century, St Stephens Plain had been at the heart of the new kind of shopping based on large department stores with plate glass windows that shifted the centre of gravity from individual specialist shops of the kind seen around the marketplace.

This area suffered badly in the Baedeker bombing raids. Some buildings, like the fifteenth-century Boar's Head, could have been restored but the prevailing postwar mood was to get rid of the old and so the opportunity was taken to demolish the entire south side of St Stephens Street. This resulted in what the architecture critic, Ian

The Old Boar's Head on St Stephen's Street. Author's collection.

Nairn, thought was 'probably the worst thing of its kind I have ever seen in what passes for a cultured city.'

Red Lion Street, the road on the north side of St Stephens Plain, had already been widened at the very end of the nineteenth century in order to accommodate the new electric trams, whose city hub was in Orford Place. Built in 1900, the south side of Red Lion Street was comprised of buildings designed by the two titans of late Victorian Norwich architecture – George Skipper and Edward Boardman; their street has survived far better than post-war St Stephen's Street.

St Stephen's Plain with St Stephens Street to the left of Buntings/M&S and Rampant Horse Street to the right.

On the south-west corner of St Stephens Plain stood Buntings Department Store designed in 1912 by local architect AF Scott. Although Scott is best remembered for his Neo-Gothic Baptist chapels he also promoted modern building techniques and we'll read more about these contradictory aspects on page 123. For Buntings he came up with a modern steel-framed structure with reinforced concrete floors, hidden – perhaps incongruously in view of the building's modernity – behind stone curtain-walls decorated with Adam Revival swags. Buntings Department Store was also damaged by the bombs of 1942 but its strong skeleton kept it standing and allowed it to be restored; the building (minus a corner cupola) lives on as Marks and Spencer. Opposite, the north-west corner fared less well. The Curl brothers' department store – part of which was built around the medieval Rampant Horse Inn, which gave name to the street – was destroyed in the air raids and a new department store arose from 1953 to 1956. In the 1960s the store was bought by Debenhams but still traded as 'Curls' until the 1970s. Now that Debenhams has closed the future of the building is unclear.

To the west, Rampant Horse Street merges into Theatre Street, the site of **Theatre Plain** – the epicentre of Georgian gentility in Chapel Fields. An advertisement placed by dance master Francis Noverre gives the address of his first annual ball as being in the Assembly Rooms on Playhouse Plain. Theatre Plain was therefore outside the Assembly House, not the Theatre Royal next door as confirmed on Millard and Manning's map of 1830. Somewhat ironically for a city claiming to have plains instead of squares, *White's Directory* of 1845 refers to the space as Theatre Square. At last a square. This may be because we were now in an age when squares – unlike the irregular medieval spaces where streets collided – had been made fashionable by the development of urban squares in Georgian London. As

we'll see on page 44 there would be no Georgian new town in Norwich and so the Assembly House and the Theatre Royal – both designed by local architect Thomas Ivory – together with Chapelfield Gardens, was the closest this city came to a Georgian enclave.

St Giles' Plain. The provisional nature of some of the Norwich plains is apparent from Richard Lane's book *The Plains of Norwich*. *White's Directory* of 1845 does not, he writes, list St Giles' Plain in the street guide despite several traders giving their address there. Nor could I find it on the 1884 OS map, the Millard and Manning 1830 map, Cole's 1807 and King's 1766. This is not to say that the plain didn't exist but that locals were more ready than mapmakers to apply the local name for these awkward spaces.

The church stands above Cow Hill, where St Giles Street elides into Upper St Giles. The area outside the church would have looked more tranquil before the 1970s when Cleveland Street joined the plain, bringing traffic off the Grapes Hill roundabout and the Inner Link Road.

Until the Conquest, the settlement's main axis ran north-south, from Magdalen Street, through Tombland, to King Street. The Normans changed this by developing the French Borough westwards from their Castle and Marketplace. Two Norman streets from the market

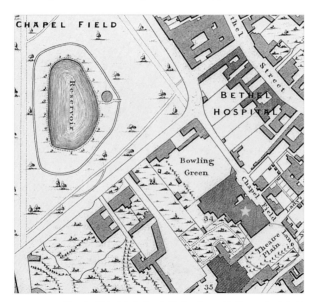

Theatre Plain (circled) outside the Assembly Rooms (red star). Theatre Royal, yellow star. Millard & Manning's map (1830). Photo: the author. Courtesy of Norfolk County Council.

St Giles Church, and Plain, from Bethel Street

converged at St Giles: Lower Newport (now St Giles Street) and Upper Newport (now Bethel, formerly Bedlam, Street).

Dominating the plain is Great St Giles, situated on a hill 85 feet above sea level. If you were to stand on top of the magnificent church tower you would be 205 feet above the sea, not as tall as the county's high point (Beeston Bump, 344 feet), but still dizzyingly high for Norfolk. Two thirds up the tower the single clock-face points down St Giles' Street to the Guildhall, next to the marketplace. The solitary hour hand on a dial of ten-feet diameter should have been easy to see at a distance although visibility – and more precise time-keeping required in the railway age – was improved in the mid-nineteenth century when the hour hand was supplemented by a six and a half feet minute-hand.

Churchman House

Facing the south side of the church, across the plain, is Churchman House built in 1727 for alderman Thomas Churchman and remodelled in 1751 by his son Sir Thomas. For two years (1875-7) Churchman House was the first home of the Norwich School for Girls before it moved to the Assembly House, then in 1933 to its present location on Newmarket Road. After the girls moved out, the house was bought by Dr Peter Eade, sheriff and three times mayor. Dr Eade was Chief Physician at the Norfolk and Norwich Hospital on St Stephen's Road. He was also first President of the Norwich Medico-Chirurgical Society at a time when meetings would be held on the night of a full moon to help members return home safely.

Dr Eade was also embroiled in the affair of Sir Thomas Browne's skull, which we will come to in the next chapter. Briefly, physician and philosopher Thomas Browne, the city's most famous citizen of the seventeenth century, was buried in the chancel of St Peter Mancroft. Somehow, his skull ended up in the Norfolk and Norwich Hospital Museum where, despite numerous requests for its return, it stayed until 1922. As a physician, Eade is thought to have fought against the restoration of the skull, yet it was Eade the mayor who championed the commission for Browne's statue, which was installed in the Haymarket in 1905.

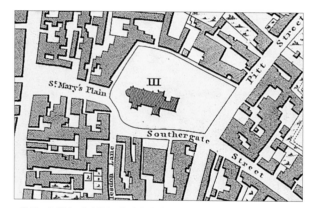

St Mary's Plain, Oak St to the left, Duke St to the right. Millard & Manning's map (1830. Photo: the author. Courtesy of Norfolk County Council

St Mary's Plain feels more of an open space than others in Norwich-over-the-Water, possibly because of the elbow room borrowed from the large churchyard.

The plain takes its name from St Mary-at-Coslany, Coslany (or island with reeds) being one of the four original Anglo-Saxon settlements on which the city is based. On the belfry, the double openings with the recessed shaft reveal the church's Anglo-Saxon origins. It is probably the oldest in Norwich.

St Mary's Church with Sexton, Son and Everard shoe factory to the left.

Until the late1800s the area consisted of 'noxious courts and alleys' but all this was to change dramatically in the following century. Norwich-over-the-Water housed many light-industrial factories and was bombed several times during the Baedeker Raids. A week after war was declared in 1939, fire swept through the nearby Baptist church but this was not caused by enemy action, just a foretaste of what was to come. Rebuilt to the original design, the church was opened again a year later but in June 1942 was completely gutted, this time as a result of enemy action. The church we see today was opened in July 1951.

The shape of the plain had changed in the 1920s. Then, old slum dwellings were demolished to make way for St Mary's Works, home to Sexton, Son and Everard, one of the city's large shoe-making factories. But it, too, was extensively damaged in 1942 by the summer bombing campaign. Although the building was restored the business closed in 1976 and the site awaits redevelopment.

The 1942 raids also claimed medieval Pykerell's House, named after an early sixteenth century sheriff and three-times mayor. Extensively restored, it is one of only six thatched houses left in Norwich. Surprisingly, I can find

no reports that its adjoining but unthatched neighbour – Zoar Strict and Particular Chapel – suffered any damage in the blaze. In evading the Luftwaffe's incendiary bombs the church was echoing its biblical namesake, Zoar, one of the five cities of the plain (the Dead Sea Plain) to escape the fire and brimstone that destroyed Sodom and Gomorrah.

Pykerell's House

LATER PLAINS

The majority of the city's plains are legacies of the medieval street plan but in the mid-1960s the term was revived to describe the site for which Sir Denys Lasdun designed the first phase of the University of East Anglia, on **University Plain**.

UEA Central Court 1990 © georgeplunkett.co.uk

The Forum in the city centre, which contains the Millennium Library, is located in **Millennium Plain** and extends our use of the Dutch loan-word into the twenty-first century.

When the Norfolk and Norwich hospital – designed by local Georgian architect Thomas Ivory with later additions by Edward Boardman – closed and the new hospital erected in the suburb of Colney (2001), the site was redeveloped as a residential estate, **Fellowes Plain**. William Fellowes (1706-1775) was a wealthy and philanthropic squire from Shotesham Hall who, after founding in his village what may have been the first cottage hospital, was the prime mover in establishing a county hospital in Norwich (founded 1771).

Within Fellowes Plain are three open spaces, all named 'plain' in their own right. The first is **Kenneth McKee Plain**, dedicated to Ken McKee CBE (1906-1991), orthopaedic surgeon at the N&N who pioneered the total hip replacement.

The second is **Edward Jodrell Plain**, named for the Jodrell family of Bayfield Hall, near Holt, who were benefactors to the old Norfolk and Norwich Hospital. Jodrell's son Alfred Jodrell sent baskets of fruit and vegetables each week to the hospital and at Christmas gave 40 oven-ready chickens and the same number of turkeys.

The third is the large green known as **Phillipa Flowerday Plain**. Before being employed by Colmans at their Carrow Works, Phillipa Flowerday (1846-1930) trained and worked as a nurse at the N&N. In 1872, she was employed at Colman's to visit the families of the workpeople as well as assisting the doctor in their dispensary. Phillipa is therefore celebrated as the first industrial nurse in the country.

IN SEARCH OF
THOMAS BROWNE'S GARDEN HOUSE

Knighted by King Charles II in St Andrew's Hall, Sir Thomas Browne (1605-1682) was probably Norwich's most famous inhabitant of the seventeenth century. He was born in London, the son of a silk merchant and, after being educated in Oxford, Padua, Montpellier and Leiden, settled in Norwich where he practiced as a physician until he died. Then there was the controversy over his skull.

In a time before knowledge was segregated into disciplines, Thomas Browne was famed as a polymath whose writings reveal an inquisitive mind that explored subjects as diverse as: the fault line between his training as a physician and the Christian faith (in *Religio Medici*, 1643); his debunking of myths and falsehoods (*Pseudodoxia Epidemica*, 1646); the incidence of the number five in patterns in nature (*The Garden of Cyrus*, 1658); and his celebrated and lyrical musings about death, prompted by the discovery of funerary urns in a Norfolk field (*Hydriotaphia, or Urne-Buriall*, 1658).

This was in the long period after the loosening of religious ties when modern science was allowed – somewhat diffidently – to get into its stride. The scientific method promoted by Sir Francis Bacon (1561-1626) involved framing hypotheses based on observations viewed through the filter of scepticism. In his book, Vulgar Errors (*Pseudodoxia Epidemica*), Browne turned a sceptical eye on such folkloric myths as: does a carbuncle give off light in the dark and, do dead kingfishers make good weathervanes? He even attended the trial in Bury St Edmunds of two women who were hanged for witchcraft. But the Enlightenment had barely got going and the proto-scientist Browne found himself straddling two worlds that had yet to drift apart – even Sir Isaac Newton sought the philosopher's stone that would turn base metal into gold.

My first encounter with Sir Thomas was when I was trying to understand how plant cells and other solid bodies pack together without leaving gaps. Another scientist, Stephen Hales (1677-1761), had provided some insight. By compressing pea seed in a pot, then counting the number of flat faces impressed onto each seed by its neighbours, Hales came up with the number 12. You can make a 12-sided dodecahedron by joining together 12 regular pentagons. This is one of Plato's 'ideal' solid bodies composed of identical faces. There are only five such bodies; a cube is one of them, made of six identical squares. The standard soccer ball is not an ideal Platonic shape for it is made by stitching together a mixture of pentagons and hexagons. In real life, the shapes of plant cells are also far from perfect. They are not made of 12 pentagonal sides as Stephen Hales reported for his

Thomas Browne. Courtesy of St Peter Mancroft

squashed peas; instead they tend *on average* to be 14-sided and each side tends, on average, to be a pentagon but sometimes they are hexagons, heptagons, octagons. Nevertheless, following the trail of fiveness took me back a further century to fellow citizen Thomas Browne.

In his book The Garden of Cyrus or The Quincuncial Lozenge (1658) Browne developed his ideas about the quincunx – the X-shape with four points forming a square or rectangle with a fifth point in the centre.

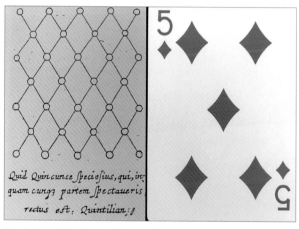

Frontispiece of The Garden of Cyrus or The Quincuncial Lozenge (1658) (left).

Cyrus, the founder of the first Persian Empire, is believed to have based the optimal-spacing lattice for planting trees on the quincunx. Browne saw this pattern throughout nature: he saw the quincunx on pineapples and the cones of fir and pine. In ragweed and oak he also noted that successive leaves emerged from the growing point in a spiral, with every fifth lined up along the stem. These were – before the word – explorations into phyllotaxis or the pattern in which leaves are arranged around the stem (paired, alternating, spiral). Now, more than 300 years later, the spiral pattern is known to be far more complex than the quincunx. Browne may not have been correct but he was there in the first flush of modern science and deserves credit for offering a mathematical basis for patterns in nature.

Many of the words from Sir Thomas Browne's writings have found their way into the Oxford English Dictionary; indeed, he stands 25th in the list of contributors. 'Retromingent' – for peeing backwards – never made it into the OED but many others did, including:

> *electricity, pubescent, polarity, prototype, rhomboidal, archetype, flammability, follicle, hallucination, coma, deductive, misconception, botanical, incontrovertible, approximate, and an early example of 'computer'.*

Despite the scepticism required of a follower of Sir Francis Bacon, and 'the scandal of my profession', Browne remained a convinced Christian who examined his spiritual beliefs in his most famous book, *Religio Medici.* He was surprisingly tolerant for his time. In

Title page of Religio Medici (1642). Houghton Library, Harvard University.

the first unauthorised edition of *Religio Medici* (The Religion of a Physician) in 1642, Browne expressed unorthodox religious ideas including the extension of toleration to infidels and those of other faiths. When the authorised version appeared the following year some of the controversial views had been excised but this didn't prevent the book being placed on the papal prohibited list.

Browne's major works were written in Norwich, at his house near St Peter Mancroft, close to the Norman marketplace. In 1671, the royal court of King Charles II came to the city. The diarist and gardener John Evelyn – who designed a pleasure garden off King Street for the future Sixth Duke of Norfolk – was part of the royal entourage and after visiting Browne wrote, 'His whole house and garden is a Paradise & Cabinet of rarities, & that of the best collection, especially Medails, books, Plants, natural things' ... 'amongst other curiosities, a collection of the Eggs of all the foule & birds he could procure ... as Cranes, Storkes ... & variety of waterfoule'. What Evelyn saw was the first attempt at listing the birds of Norfolk.

Browne's house was demolished in 1842 and a green plaque tells us that it stood approximately where Pret a Manger is now housed in George Skipper's Haymarket Chambers, at the junction with Orford Place. Historian AD Bayne wrote that 'Sir Thomas Browne is supposed to have lived in the last house of the southern end of the Gentleman's Walk, where the Savings Bank now stands'.

Haymarket Chambers 1896. © RIBA Collections

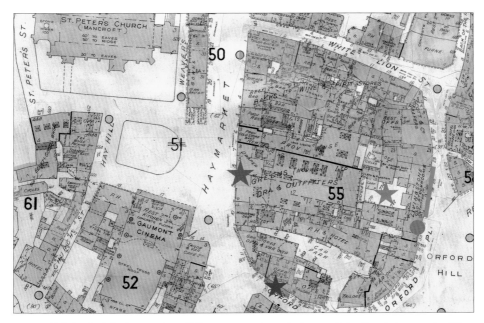

Norwich Union Goad (fire insurance) map 1949. Courtesy Aviva. Green star to green circle = Green's drapers and outfitters. Blue star = 3-5 Orford Place, site of Thomas Browne's house. Red bar = Livingstone's Temperance Hotel, bought by Greens. Red star = site of Browne's garden house.

But the Norfolk and Norwich Savings Bank stood in the way of progress and was demolished around 1900 so that the new electric trams could glide around the corner into the hub at Orford Place. Skipper designed the curved frontage of Haymarket Chambers so that the trams could turn the corner. This corner-cutting is shown on the 1949 fire map that we'll bear in mind while trying to figure out where Browne's garden house lingered until 1961.

According to George Plunkett, photographer of twentieth century Norwich, the demolition of numbers 3-5 Orford Place (blue star on map) in 1956, was marked with a stone declaring this to have been the site of Thomas Browne's house. George Plunkett placed Browne's timber-framed garden house some distance from the main building. He wrote, 'only the peak of its tall attic gable (was) visible above the roof of the adjacent Lamb Inn'. So it couldn't have been in Lamb Inn Yard, just behind the former site of Browne's house.

Later, Green's the drapers and outfitters (green star), whose main shop faced the Haymarket, opened a branch (green circle) next door to the Livingstone Temperance Hotel (red bar) in Orford Place. Green's shop, which ran from Haymarket through to Orford

Green's outfitters, Orford Place frontage 1959.
Courtesy of Norfolk County Council Library and Information Service

Thomas Browne's Garden House, drawn in 1950. © Noël Spencer. From Norwich Drawings by Noël Spencer.

After I posted this article on my blog in the summer of 2020, an Assistant Curator at Strangers' Hall Museum corroborated this location, mentioning that two of Browne's Garden House doors in the museum were recorded as being given by 'Messrs Littlewood' 1961. Also, 'lying behind former Livingstone Hotel, Castle Street; part of premises of Messrs Green, outfitter 9 and 10 Haymarket.'

To supplement his home garden Sir Thomas paid the Cathedral 10 shillings per annum for the use of a plot of land known as Browne's Meadow: 'A meadow I use in this city, beset about with sallows (willows)'. In his fascinating *Adventures of Sir Thomas Browne in the 21st Century*, Hugh Aldersey-Williams wrote that

Place, was demolished in 1961 to make way for a Littlewoods Department Store (now the site of Primark), but not before leaving us an eye-witness description of Browne's Garden House.

Thomas Browne's main house disappeared long before modern ideas of preservation, but the destruction of his garden house as recently as 1961 now seems unforgivable for this was the botanical garden admired by John Evelyn and the object of pilgrimage by Fellows of the nascent Royal Society. Our Protestant Dutch refugees – who held annual competitions called Florists' Feasts – had imported a love of plant breeding and it would be surprising if, in such an environment, Browne's garden was restricted to medicinal plants. What a loss to garden history.

In 1950, the Head of the School of Art, Noël Spencer, visited Greens when they 'were using the Livingstone as a shop and, while making a purchase there (i.e., Green's Orford Place branch), I noticed an ancient building in the yard behind, and obtained permission to draw it.' This would place Thomas Browne's Garden House in the yard marked with a red star on the map.

Browne's Meadow on the south side of Cathedral Close

Browne 'let it go', to see what would grow if untended. After Browne died, the ground was used to produce vegetables for the Cathedral, then it was used as allotments for residents of Cathedral Close, now it is a car park.

Sir Thomas Browne died on the 19th October 1682. One suggestion is that he died after eating too plentifully of a venison feast but others believe this was out of character for such an abstemious man. He was buried in the chancel of St Peter Mancroft, some 200 yards from his house. There he lay until 1840 when workmen are said to have broken the lid of the lead coffin with a pickaxe while digging the grave of Mrs. Bowman, wife of the then Vicar of St. Peter Mancroft. Mr Fitch, a local antiquarian, was suspiciously close at hand and it is not clear whether the desecration was accidental or deliberate. Either way, the sexton, George Potter, removed the skull and some hair. The skull came into the possession of the surgeon, Edward Lubbock, upon whose death it passed to the old Norwich and Norfolk Hospital Museum on St Stephen's Road. Despite requests from the church, the skull remained on display at the hospital and was only reunited with Browne's bones in 1922.

Sir Thomas's coffin plate, which had broken in two during attempts to remove it, had also been 'mislaid'. One half of this 7x6 inch brass plate lies with other Browne memorabilia in a glass case in the St Nicholas Chapel of St Peter Mancroft. A contemporary impression of the coffin plate revealed an inscription probably composed by Browne's eldest son Edward, physician to Charles II, and President of the College of Physicians: 'With the dust of this alchemical body he converts lead into gold' – something that even the great Sir Isaac Newton could not achieve.

In 1905 the city commemorated its adopted son by unveiling a statue equidistant between Sir Thomas Browne's house and church. From his vantage point above the old hay market, Browne holds the base of a

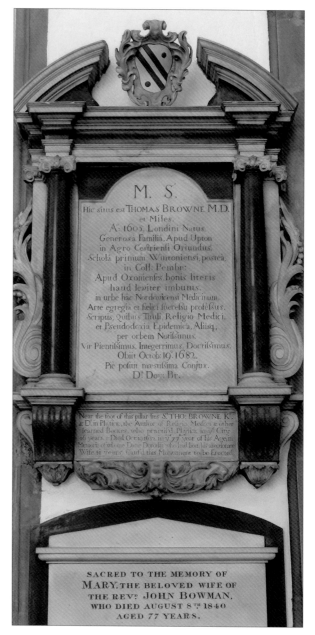

Sir Thomas Browne's wall monument in St Peter Mancroft, above his burial place in the chancel. The lower panel commemorates Mary Bowman who disturbed Browne's bones.

Henry Pegram's statue of Browne contemplating a funerary urn, 1905.

Romano-British funerary urn and meditates on death. This relates to his book, *Urn Burial* (1658), in which he explored thoughts prompted by the discovery of urns in a field some 12 miles north of Norwich. The urns, dug up by Sir Robert Paston in the parish of Brampton near his Oxnead Park, contained ashes along with coins that may have paid the ferryman .

Browne's words were prescient, '... who knows the fate of his bones, or how often he is to be buried? Who hath the oracles of his ashes, or whither they are to be scattered? ... To be gnawed out of our graves, to have our skulls made drinking-bowls, and our bones turned into pipes to delight and sport our enemies, are tragical abominations.'

A postscript on Thomas Browne's knighthood

Ambiguity surrounds the circumstances of Thomas Browne's knighthood. In 1671 King Charles II and his court came to Norwich where he stayed at the Duke of Norfolk's Palace off present-day Duke Street (requiring the famous indoor tennis court to be converted into kitchens). The corporation paid £900 for a sumptuous banquet at the New Hall (now St Andrew's Hall) after which the king conferred honours.

According to some accounts Browne was unexpectedly knighted when the mayor, 'earnestly begged to be refused' and, as in pass-the-parcel, the honour moved along the line. This played to the idea that a promiscuous monarch with several mistresses was as free in conferring honours as he was lax in his private life. Confirmation of the monarch's largesse came within 24 hours when King Charles knighted 13-year-old Henry Hobart at Blickling. But Browne was a distinguished thinker and this version of events ignores the great respect in which he was held in this and other countries. The historian Philip Browne (1814) gave a plain account that rings more true: 'After dinner his majesty conferred the knighthood on Dr Thomas Browne, one of the most learned and worthy persons of the age. The mayor, Thomas Thacker esq. declined the honour'.

Inside the walls of a city known for its green spaces, Norwich's largest public park has been variously known as Chapel-in-the-Fields, Chapel Fields, Chapple/ Chapply/Chaply/Chapley Field, and now Chapelfield Gardens; my daughters call it Chappy. It can be traced back to John le Brun who in 1250 founded the Chapel of the Blessed Virgin Mary in the Fields. This evolved into the College of St Mary in the Fields, part of which was to be incorporated into the Georgian Assembly House (1745-6).

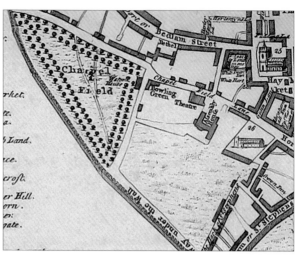

Samuel King's map 1766 showing Churchman's triangular walk.
Photo: the author, courtesy of Norfolk County Council

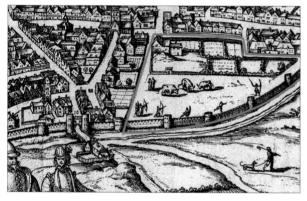

Braun and Hogenberg's Plan of Norwich 1581.
Photo: the author, courtesy of Norfolk County Council.

Braun and Hogenberg's prospect of the city of Norwich (1581) is based on Cuningham's map of 1558 and so provides a glimpse of Chapel Field not long after Henry VIII's Dissolution of the Monasteries (1536-1541); the city took ownership in 1569. The map shows this sector of the city dominated by two areas of open ground: the land behind Chapel Field House and a triangular meadow grazed by cows and occupied by figures with bows and arrows. This was at a time when it was still compulsory for men between the ages of 15 and 60 to prepare for war and we see them practicing archery under the walls. But warfare was changing and by the latter part of the century the field became the mustering ground for the city's trained artillerymen.

By the time of King's map of 1766 the two parts were still largely open ground. Only minor inroads had been made by the bowling green, the Theatre Royal and the Assembly House, which provided entertainment for leisured Georgians. On the triangular field we see the double row of elms that lessee Thomas Churchman planted for his promenade. This latter portion would survive as present-day Chapelfield Gardens.

A generation later, co-founder of the Norwich Society of Artists, John Crome (1768-1821), in his etching 'View in Chapel-Field' (not shown), depicted a scene of bucolic openness with cattle being driven down tree-lined avenues. The city had always allowed Chapelfield to be used as a public space and in 1656 had resisted Lady Hobart's attempt to prevent citizens passing through. Infilling was the norm in the rest of the city, where insanitary shanty housing was flung up in the courtyards of those wealthy enough to have escaped the waves of epidemics. But instead of revealing the realities of urban living Crome depicted the rustic tranquility of Chapelfield Gardens.

At the beginning of the eighteenth century, however, the fields were fenced in. Then in 1867 the council erected iron railings, which would be removed in World War Two, purportedly to make guns. This would have been the 'massive palisade' supplied by W S Boulton (later of Boulton & Paul) who, 'produces every kind of railing ... also mincing and sausage machines'.

Chapelfield Gardens lies in the crook of the protective arm provided by the city walls, built about 1300. Some 500 years later the gates at its southern and western extremities were demolished to ease the passage of horse-drawn traffic: St Giles' Gate in 1792 and St Stephen's Gate a year later. The ancient walls were disappearing too, signifying a loosening of the hold of the medieval past and allowing – if only notionally – the removal of noxious air. In the 1860s, some of the wall around Chapelfield was used as hardcore for the new Prince of Wales Road, built to connect the markets around the castle with the newly arrived railway. Other parts of the 'Chapelfield' boundary were protected by the presence of houses that had been built against the wall – some with windows knocked through to give a view of the gardens – but these houses would be demolished in 1969 to make way for the ring road.

JH Gurney's fountain and obelisk in Tombland

City Wall outside Chapelfield Gardens after demolition of attached houses in 1969 ©georgeplunkett.co.uk

King's map of 1766 shows a water house within Churchman's triangular walk, part of the corporation's scheme to supply water to the city. Water pumped from the river at New Mills (near Westwick Street, upstream of the built-up area) supplied Chapelfield and Tombland. The Tombland works were described in 1698 by the traveller Celia Fiennes as 'a great well house with a wheele to wind up the water ... a large pond walled up with brick a mans height ... (and) a water house to supply the town by pipes'. This is commemorated by John Henry Gurney's obelisk and fountain of 1850 that, after the cholera epidemic of 1849, replaced an old insanitary water cistern. Gurney's memorial was moved a few yards in the recent (2021) transformation of Tombland.

Provision of unfiltered water was restricted to a few parts of the city, and then only to those who would pay for the connection. In 1792, supply was taken over by the Norwich Waterworks Company who built the water tower and reservoir in Chapel Field that appear on Millard and Manning's map of 1830. The presence of waterworks in Chapelfield had sullied the illusion of a bosky retreat where Georgian gentility could associate and by 1840 the park had become 'the resort of loose and idle boys' and washerwomen. One idea had been to dignify the site by placing a statue of Nelson on an island in the middle of the reservoir. This never

happened and the statue was located instead in the cathedral's Upper Close.

By 1852, the Waterworks Company had built a new reservoir in Lakenham and agreed to hand over Chapelfield Gardens to the corporation provided it was laid out as a public garden. Houses had already been built up against the outer face of the city walls but by designating Chapelfield Gardens a public park it was now formally protected from building within its boundaries.

In 1866 the corporation offered the north-west corner of Chapelfield Gardens to the militia for building a drill hall – an echo of the archery practice depicted on the sixteenth century maps. This castellated Neo-Gothic building, designed by the City Surveyor, Ernest Benest, incorporated part of a semi-circular tower from the old city wall. The triangular shape of Chapelfield Gardens would be lost when this corner was flattened beneath the inner link road of 1968-1975. The drill hall itself was demolished in 1963 but the position of the old city-wall tower incorporated into its structure is commemorated by a semi-circle of cobbles on the Grapes Hill roundabout. To connect this roundabout with incoming traffic from Earlham Road – which had previously been continuous with St Giles Street – an awkward fiddler's

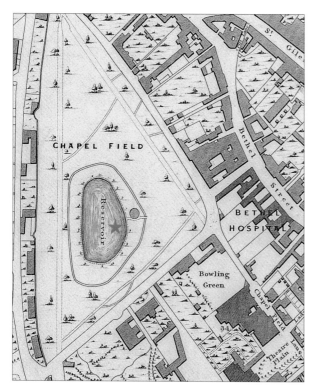

Millard and Manning's map 1830, showing reservoir in Chapelfield Gardens.
Photo: the author, courtesy of Norfolk County Council

Volunteer Drill Hall 1866-1963 incorporating part of semi-circular tower from the city wall. ©georgeplunkett.co.uk

elbow was created by diverting vehicles a little way up Unthank Road. Traffic was reconnected with St Giles Street via a spur off the roundabout, creating Cleveland Road in the process. It probably made sense at the time.

Inside the gardens, one of its most exotic inhabitants was the iron pavilion designed by Thomas Jeckyll. Made by Barnard Bishop and Barnards at their Norfolk Ironworks, and with much of the bas-relief work being forged by Aquila Eke (George Plunkett's great uncle), it won a gold medal at the Philadelphia exhibition of 1876. Four years later it was bought by the Norwich corporation for £500 and installed in Chapelfield Gardens. I've written at length about Aesthetic Jeckyll and his Japanese-influenced designs for Barnards' Norfolk Iron Works, so I won't run on, but this was the famous 'Pagoda', enclosed by railings in the form of uber-fashionable sunflowers – here, in provincial Norwich. Yet, despite it being an icon of the Aesthetic Movement and a triumph of Norwich craftsmanship, the modernists who created the City of Norwich Plan for 1945 judged the Pagoda to be dispensable and so it was demolished in 1949. As Gavin Stamp wrote in *Lost*

Grapes Hill roundabout.
The yellow line tracks the old city wall; the magnified curve shows the pattern of pebbles marking the city wall tower built into the drill hall. © John Fielding

The pagoda next to the bandstand in Chapelfield Gardens, early twentieth century. Author's collection.

Victorian Britain, 'Victorian, quite simply, was a term of abuse' during the post-war period.

Another Victorian occupant of Chapelfield Gardens was a thatched teahouse, known as King Prempeh's Bungalow, built about the time of the Ashanti campaign in West Africa. Prempeh the First (1870-1931), who had tried to negotiate an honourable peace with the British, was captured by an expeditionary force led by Robert (*'Scouting for Boys'*) Baden-Powell and sent into exile. In 1902, the Ashanti Kingdom became part of the Gold Coast colony. Prempeh, once the ruler of all he surveyed, was eventually released into a British protectorate of which he found himself Chief Scout.

Between 1800 and 1850 Norwich's population had doubled and the once-rural hamlet of Heigham to the west had expanded up to the city walls. From about 1815 a New City arose on the south-west side of Chapelfield Road. This signalled the start of the expansion of working-class housing away from the insanitary muddle of the old city. In South Heigham a piece of land once used as a market garden became Crook's Place and, along with Union Place and Julian Place, these terraces of small houses were built to accommodate an influx of workers from the countryside. Mostly back-to-back, these modest dwellings had shared privies and water pumps but were prevented by strict covenants from possessing pig sties. Still, the small houses proved to be insanitary and were demolished during rounds of twentieth century slum clearance. A generation later, terraced housing on the Steward and Unthank estates was built to higher standards and continued the city's southwestward expansion well beyond the pull of the medieval walls.

Chapelfield North, which bounds the gardens to the north, is architecturally rich. The street itself hasn't altered significantly during my 40 years in the city though the ebb and flow of its traffic has changed according to various schemes. One bystander that has overseen a more dramatic change in transport fashion

Howes & Sons Ltd in Chapelfield North, early twentieth century.
Photo: howesfamilies.com

is The Garage, originally built as the new motor works for Howes & Sons Ltd and now a centre for performing arts. When the firm was established as coach builders in 1784 they were manufacturing four-wheeled carriages like their 'light boat-shaped barouche' but the early twentieth century saw them on the cusp of a revolutionary change in personal transport. While the photograph shows 'Motor Engineers' on the right-hand side of the main entrance, the phrase 'Coach Builders' on the left refers to a not quite vanished age when 'coachwork' referred to the bodywork of horse-drawn vehicles.

A twentieth century addition to Chapelfield North is the Norwich Spiritualist Church. Built by RG Carter in 1936, this single-storey building was part-funded by proceedings from a post-World War Two spiritualist meeting addressed by the faith's most famous adherent, Sir Arthur Conan Doyle.

The third side of the triangle of streets around Chapelfield Gardens is Chapelfield East, which divides the gardens from the larger block that once housed Caley's chocolate factory (later, Rowntree Mackintosh then Nestlé). Demolished to make way for the Chapelfield Shopping Centre (2005) this complex was – with a nod to its ecclesiastical heritage – recently renamed Chantry Place.

In 1505 and 1507 great fires swept away the majority of Norwich's early medieval buildings and a new city, still largely timber-framed, arose on the old street plan. Two centuries later, as historian Marc Girouard noted of the country in general, Georgian buildings were raised, 'on medieval plots and incorporated a medieval, or at least Tudor, structure behind their new facades'. Grafting new faces onto old frames was therefore not peculiar to Norwich; however, the lack of stone, in what was still the nation's second city, meant that new classically-influenced buildings based on proportion and balance would be of red brick or plasterwork masquerading as stone. The straitjacket of a medieval street-plan, confined for much of the Georgian period within the city walls, meant that no grand squares and sweeping crescents would be laid out, as in London, Bath, Edinburgh, Newcastle and Bristol. There would be no Georgian new town in Norwich.

Georgianisation is everywhere in central Norwich. Most commonly, older timber-framed buildings were brought up to date by the addition of a Classical door surround and sash windows. Less commonly, the over-sailing of upper floors was made flush by the addition of a new facade, disguising the timber-frame beneath. In 1714, on her travels by side saddle, Celia Fiennes astutely noticed the less than thoroughgoing modernisation of the medieval city. She commented on the lack of brick buildings in the city centre, noting that what few she saw belonged to rich merchants in Norwich-over-the-Water. '... but all their buildings are of an old form, mostly in deep poynts and much tileing as has been observ'd before, and they playster on Laths wch they strike out into squares like broad free stone on ye outside, wch makes their fronts Look pretty well; and some they build high and Contract ye roofes resembling the London houses, but none of brick Except some few beyond the river wch are built of some of ye Rich factors like ye London buildings'.

House in Pottergate altered in C18

The faking of plaster by adding grooves to make the material appear like courses of rusticated stone is nicely illustrated by the building at the top of Elm Hill. Mr James Reeves' house was made about 1619 but by the time of Cobridge's 'Mapp of the City of Norwich' (1727) it had been given an unconvincing Georgian makeover. Cobridge's subscribers who wanted their house to be

James Reeves' building at the corner of Elm Hill and Princes Street

depicted in the margins of the map were asked to pay seven shillings down and three on delivery. Mr Reeve should regard this as ten bob well spent for, although most churches remain, his is the only domestic house that can still be recognised. Paradoxically, Mr Reeve's house is the least grandiose of the illustrated buildings and we can only mourn the number of large seventeenth and eighteenth century houses that we have lost.

St Giles Street, south side

During the eighteenth century, most of the houses in Norwich-over-the-Water were remodelled or rebuilt, no doubt on profits from a thriving textile industry, and fine examples can be seen along Colegate. Perhaps the most imposing 'Georgian' thoroughfare in the city is St Giles Street, full of houses either built in the Georgian

period or brought up to date with a new facade perhaps raised in order to approach classical proportions. None of the newly-built brick houses of the 1700s retained the old courtyard plan of Gothic buildings. Abandoned by the rich then filled with the shanties of the poor, numerous 'courts' or 'yards' were to become insanitary slums that lasted well into the twentieth century. The wealthy either retreated to their country houses surrounding the city or lived in their new, fashionable townhouses. The wealthy master-weaver Thomas Harvey did both. He built a mansion in parkland just north of the city, Catton House, while maintaining a town house in the heart of the weaving district. This was number 18 Colegate, built in the early eighteenth century. (Thomas Harvey was the man whose collection of Dutch paintings influenced the co-founder of the Norwich Society of Artists, John Crome, who lived off Colegate). In their Norwich volume of *The Buildings of England*, Pevsner and Wilson considered 18 Colegate to be '(one) of the best early C18 houses in Norwich' and awarded a similar accolade to Churchman's House on St Giles Plain – 'one of the finest houses in Norwich'. The imposing front we see today was added in 1751 by Sir Thomas Churchman in the course of remodelling his father's house. Both this and Harvey's house are seven-bayed but the pediment above the central three bays of Churchman's House adds a more elegant top note.

Harvey's House, 18 Colegate

Churchman House, St Giles Plain

As we saw in the previous chapter, it was Churchman who, in 1746, planted a triangular walk of elms in Chapel Field – the area leased from the council, behind his house. This was the age of the promenade in which polite society paraded itself in the evening, or the afternoon in winter. In the provinces, polite society was mainly composed of the rising middling sort who may well have arrived at gentility in one bound. Promenaders would take the air in their finery but, in this Second City passeggiata, their position in the social order would be established by a warm greeting or a curt nod. In 1777, Parson Woodforde, whose diary tells us so much about Georgian Norwich, ' …went and drank tea this evening … with Mrs. Davy in St. Stephen's Parish, with her, Mrs. Roupe, her mother-in-law and a very

Norwich Post founded 1701, Redwell Street

pretty young Lady from the boarding School. We took a walk afterwards in Chapel Field etc.'

In addition to drinking tea or coffee with friends, the leisured class could visit one of the several coffee houses around the marketplace. There, they could read newspapers, gossip and – as unwitting participants in the English Enlightenment – discuss ideas that might have been considered seditious in the sixteenth and seventeenth centuries. An Act of Parliament that restricted printing to London, Oxford and Cambridge had been allowed to lapse in 1695 and in 1701 the Norwich Post appeared as the first truly provincial newspaper. By 1707, when only about six newspapers had established themselves in the provinces, Norwich had three. This was accompanied by a surge in the number of booksellers, which rose to 17 by the end of the Regency (1820).

The east side of the marketplace was where the fashionable came to gaze into the windows of specialist stores along Gentleman's Walk – an early shopping parade. Shops along the Walk included: Lammas Bros (tea dealers); Potter & Co (furrier); Sidney & Ladyman (tea dealers); W Ringer (Berlin [wool embroidery] and fancy repository). Other shops included confectioners, glove makers, coffee roasters, china dealers, mercers specialising in lace, hatters and booksellers.

From 1724, advertisements in the local newspaper invited Members and 'Clubbers' to listen to professional musicians at the Musick Night in Mr Freemoult's Long Room. There was also music and dancing at assemblies, especially during Assize Week in early August, when county society came to town. The genteel could visit pleasure gardens, country cousins of London's Vauxhall and Ranelagh Gardens. At Quantrell's pleasure garden, for instance, the interval at concerts could be filled with humorous dialogues and songs, the evening completed with a celebration of military victories animated with illuminations, transparencies, capped off with spectacular fireworks.

The days needed filling too. Visiting lecturers would expound on a range of advances in the natural sciences for this was the Age of Reason and the enlightened were hungry for Knowledge as well as Diversion. In one day in 1785 Parson Woodforde explored the two poles: he attended a lecture at the Assembly House on astronomy aided by a large mechanical orrery and in the afternoon he 'went and saw the learned Pigg at the rampant Horse in St Stephens'.

The Octagon Chapel, Colegate

Provided they pledged an oath of allegiance, nonconformists were extended the freedom of worship by the Act of Toleration (1689). In the following century a new nonconformist chapel arose on Colegate – a manifestation of the strong current of dissent that ran through the city. Initially, Robert Brettingham was engaged as architect and surveyor but seems to have been discharged by a select committee. Thomas Ivory (1709-1799) then competed for the contract, which he won, aided by his 'Moddle' for an octangular building. Commissioned by the Presbyterians, Ivory's new chapel of 1754-6 was said by John Wesley to be the most beautiful meeting house in Europe.

In 1751, six years after purchasing his freedom as a carpenter, 42-year-old Thomas Ivory had been appointed to do 'all the carpenter work' in the medieval Great Hospital on Bishopgate. Ivory leased land from the hospital in order to build his own house in which he lived until his death. The architect imported and exported timber from his business premises on Bishopgate and it was on this street that he built what was probably his first major project in the city – the Methodist Meeting House or Tabernacle, diagonally opposite the ancient Adam and Eve pub. His client was the Reverend James Wheatley who preached as an Independent Methodist, having been expelled by Wesley from the Methodist movement for immoral conduct. Wheatley saved the money for his church, partly one feels, for his own protection since he was assaulted for his views when he travelled the region.

Thomas Ivory's claim to have been the man who built Georgian Norwich rests largely on the Octagon Chapel and two buildings dedicated to entertainment on the Chapel Field Estate – the closest in Norwich to a Georgian enclave. There were about two dozen proprietors of the estate, ranging from local aristocracy to merchants and manufacturers, their aim being to create a superior neighbourhood for leisure. Along with a new bowling green, the remodelled assembly rooms were opened in 1755, adjacent to Churchman's triangular walk. The Assembly House was built on the vestiges of the ancient College of St Mary-in-the-Fields and Sir Henry Hobart's mansion, which was already used for occasional assemblies. This was the town house of Hobart of Blickling Hall, who had been Steward of Norwich in 1595 and went on to become Attorney General. An anonymous tourist in 1741 had pronounced, 'the buildings which have anything of grandeur in them are all Gothic' but the Assembly House is a Georgian building of which Norwich could be proud, for no other city of its size could match it, except Bath. Due to lack of funds, Ivory was unable to remodel the attached wings but this didn't prevent the connecting doors from being thrown open so that dancers could form an extended line 143 feet long.

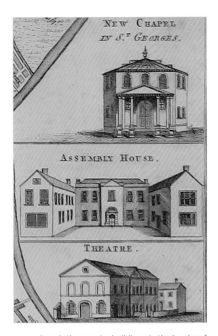

New Chapel in S.t Georges.

Assembly House.

Theatre.

Ivory's three major buildings, in the border of
Samuel King's 1776 Plan of Norwich.
Photo: the author, courtesy of Norfolk County Council

On an adjacent plot in 1757, Ivory built the 1000-seat Theatre Royal, purportedly based on the Theatre Royal Drury Lane. As proprietor, he engaged the Norwich Company of Comedians to perform plays. To get around the inconvenient fact that only London theatres could be licensed to perform plays, Ivory renamed his enterprise The Grand Concert Hall and presented free plays in the interval between the paid-for concert. After an Act of 1767 allowed the licensing of theatres outside the capital, Norwich became the second provincial theatre to receive royal assent. Ivory's theatre was not to survive. It was modified by William Wilkins in 1801 and rebuilt in 1826 by William Wilkins Jr., better known as architect of the National Gallery. Wilkins' theatre burned down in 1934.

In the 1760s, Thomas Ivory built a four-storey terrace in Surrey Street. Numbers 35/33 and 31/29 were completed ca.1761 while 27/25 were built around1773 with the possible involvement of Ivory's son William. In 1940 a stick of bombs fell in the street outside 27/25, destroying the porch. In 1963 the entire building was demolished to be replaced with a modern block. Outside number

The Assembly House

The Ivory terrace in Surrey Street; the far block is a 1960s replacement

Ivory House, All Saints Green

29 is a plaque recording that this was once home to Sir James Edward Smith, son of a wealthy Norwich textile merchant, who founded the Linnean Society and brought the Linnean Collection to this city. The collection was comprised of Carl Linnaeus's own 'type specimens' – the pressed and dried standards for each species. This was at the height of the world-wide collecting of plants and animals whose classification into ever finer groups was to pave the way for Charles Darwin's Theory of Evolution. Smith also had what must have been a fascinating garden and as a former plant scientist I flinch each time I read that the the Eastern Counties Bus Company bought the garden in the 1930s to build the new bus station.

Around the corner from the Ivory terrace on Surrey Street, Thomas built Ivory House for himself at the west end of All Saints Green, but immediately let it out in 1772 at £60 per annum to a Miles Branthwayte. From 1860, the house was to become the Norfolk Militia Artillery Barracks with sufficient land to provide for a parade ground and stables.

In 1779, Thomas Ivory died of heart disease. He is buried in Norwich Cathedral where he is commemorated by a marble wall-plaque carved by his nephew, John.

Ivory's wall monument in Norwich Cathedral. © Roland Harris

The sculpted monuments found in churches provide a remarkable public record of changes in fashion, politics and religion. The church dominated medieval life; it was where people were buried but there was no democracy in death for not all were commemorated inside the building where they had worshipped in life.

> 'But man is a Noble Animal, splendid in ashes, and pompous in the grave, solemnizing Nativities and Deaths with equal lustre ...'
>
> (Sir Thomas Browne, Urn Burial).

Until the 12th century, only clerics were allowed to be buried within the church. After this, the highborn could be represented as three-dimensional figures lying upon their tomb-chests. Here is Sir Roger de Kerdiston (1337) from Reepham, just north of Norwich. He lies casually on his cruel bed of rocks, legs are crossed as was the fashion from 1250 to 1350. Sir Roger's right hand is stretched uncomfortably across his chest to grasp his sword, as if ready to battle with death. Over the years, crossed legs have been taken to mean that the knight went on a crusade with the number of expeditions signified by where the legs were crossed (ankle, knee or thigh) but this may have been an invention of the sixteenth century.

Lady Joan and Sir Edmund de Thorp at Ashwellthorpe, Norfolk 1417

Sir Roger de Kerdiston, SS Mary and Michael Reepham

At Ashwellthorpe, Sir Edmund de Thorp and his wife Joan lie at rest, their hands at prayer. He died in Normandy fighting for Henry V. Alabaster is easier to sculpt than marble, allowing fine details of contemporary fashion to be recorded. Here, on the Thorp tomb, Dame Joan wears her hair in a reticulated headdress in which the elaborate side nets have not quite evolved into the even more fanciful horns and hearts of the coming century. And, Sir Edmund wears around his helmet a decorative circlet or torse – a trace of the rolled cloth that once provided a pad beneath the helm.

A different kind of prestige monument, a one-off, was erected in St Andrew Hingham to Thomas, Lord Morley (d. 1435), Lord of Hingham and Lord Marshall of Ireland. Made of alien red sandstone it runs from floor to ceiling on the north wall of the chancel. In their Buildings of England, Pevsner and Wilson thought it, 'one of the most impressive wall monuments of the C15 in the whole of England ... like no other.' They suggested it was based on the Erpingham Gate to Norwich Cathedral, sponsored in 1420 by Sir Thomas Erpingham, captain of the archers at Agincourt. Few possessed the lord of the manor's right, or could afford, to erect such a dominating memorial within the church.

The Morley Memorial compared with the Erpingham Gate

The impact of classically-influenced Renaissance architecture was not fully felt in England until the reign of Elizabeth I although elements of Italian Renaissance style appeared during the reign of the Tudor kings – the most famous example being Henry Tudor's tomb designed by Pietro Torrigiano and commissioned by his son, Henry VIII, for Westminster Abbey. Some of the finest early sixteenth century East Anglian tombs are in terracotta, a material made fashionable by visiting Italian craftsmen. Two of the most outstanding terracotta tombs of their type in England are to be found in St John Evangelist, Oxborough, in West Norfolk. These are in the Bedingfeld chapel that commemorates Lady Margaret Bedingfeld and her husband Sir Edmund, Marshal of Calais. Instead of the pinnacles and pointed arches of the Gothic, the numerous flat pilasters on the Bedingfeld tombs reflect the revival of Greco-Roman architecture.

The craftsmen responsible for the Bedingfeld monuments are also thought to have made the terracotta tomb-chest in Norwich's St George Colegate for Robert Jannys, mayor in 1517 and 1524. On the front of the tomb, baluster pilasters with Ionic capitals separate decorative panels in low relief, the central one bearing the merchant's mark for a man who made his money as a grocer. Stylistically, Mayor Jannys's tomb-chest bears some resemblance to the later monument (not shown) to the Third Duke of Norfolk (d 1554), premier Earl Marshal of England – the man who snatched the chain

The Jannys tomb in St George Colegate 1553/4

of office from around the neck of Thomas Cromwell. The Howards had absented themselves from Norwich and the duke's far grander tomb is not to be found in Norfolk but at St Michael's Framlingham, Suffolk. The Duke of Norfolk's memorial may be elevated above Mayor Jannys' by its superb quality and embellishment with finely-carved figures but both share the round-headed arches and balusters of the Early Renaissance.

Sir William Paston d. 1608, at St Nicholas', North Walsham.

Earlier we saw the Paston family progress from poverty to nobility. On his tomb-chest in North Walsham, Sir William Paston (d.1608) lolls with head in hand. This 'not dead, just resting' pose was mocked by Bosola in Webster's 'The Duchess of Malfi' when he said, 'Princes' images on their tombs do not lie ... seeming to pray up to heaven; but with their hands under their cheek, as if they died of the tooth-ache.' The not quite lifeless pose implies that the dead could rise again but the first explicit example of the resurrection theme in Norfolk is said to belong to Thomas Marsham (d.1638) at Stratton Strawless.

For 150 years before the Coke family built Holkham Hall, they buried their dead in the mausoleum outside the church in Tittleshall St Mary, a small village in West Norfolk. After the break with Rome the rood screen no longer marked a hard border between nave and chancel and the monuments of the titled and wealthy increasingly invaded the part of the church once reserved for the clergy. Nowhere is this better illustrated than in Tittleshall where the severity of the nave contrasts with the richness of the chancel filled with Coke monuments. The founder of the family's fortune, Sir Edward Coke, was the Lord Chancellor who

Sir Edward Coke d. 1634 in Tittleshall St Mary. Workshop of Nicholas Stone.

prosecuted the Earl of Essex, Sir Walter Raleigh, and Guy Fawkes and his co-conspirators in the Gunpowder Plot. When he was made the first Lord Chief Justice it was hoped that this independently-minded man – a staunch supporter of parliament and the common law – would bend to the will of King James I but he refused and was dismissed in 1616. He died in 1634, in the reign of King Charles I, by which time his monument is clearly Classical in style with none of the strapwork, skulls, hourglasses, scythes etc of the Jacobean period. The effigy on Sir Edward's tomb-chest depicts the man at rest, supine, hands held in prayer as he awaits resurrection; only the Four Virtues above him show signs of drowsy activity.

The Anguish Monument (d. 1617) in St George Tombland

Norwich and its freemen had long enjoyed a greater than usual degree of civic independence granted by the Crown. This, together with a shift in the balance of power brought about by the Protestant Reformation, ensured that monuments to the mercantile elite – and not just those who were high-born or had gained national prominence – started to appear in greater numbers in the city's churches. During the sixteenth century it became increasingly common to find such monuments in which a kneeling husband and wife face each other across a prayer desk with their offspring ranged behind them. Originally, the presence of kneeling figures was generally understood to mean they were praying for a speedy purging of sins and the passage to heaven but, after the rejection of the doctrine of Purgatory, the presence of weepers came to represent lineage and continuity of the family.

'Kneeler' monuments are thought to have arrived from France via The Netherlands. Norwich, home to many immigrants from the Low Countries, has some wonderful examples. In St George Tombland, secreted behind the organ, is the memorial to alderman, speaker of the council and mayor Thomas Anguish (1538-1617) at whose mayoral inauguration 33 people were crushed to death after the crowd tried to escape exploding fireworks. His monument is by Master Mason to the Crown, Nicholas Stone, who celebrates neither royalty nor aristocracy but a merchant in his red mayoral robe. Nine sons and three daughters are depicted; only the five sons not holding skulls survived the parents while two of the sons are swaddled chrysoms, who died soon after birth. Evidently, when families were large, rules of proportion and perspective had to be relaxed in order to accommodate all the children on the monument.

Instead of a high Baroque monument in marble by the fashionable London sculptor, the Anguish family seem to have chosen an old-fashioned design in alabaster, more consistent with the Jacobean work used in other of the city's mayoral monuments. Stone was paid £20, compared to the £340 he charged for Dame Katherine Paston's tomb.

The rise of the wall monument in the period following the Reformation can be seen as an unintended consequence of the puritanical whitewashing of church walls. The obliteration of brightly coloured Catholic wall paintings liberated vast acres to be colonised by wall plaques. A wonderful example can be seen at Saints Peter and Paul, Heydon, where cleaning work in 1970 revealed that wall tablets had been unwittingly placed on top of fourteenth century wall paintings. The murals illustrated the morality tale of The Three Living and The Three Dead in which three young noblemen out hunting encounter three animated corpses that reminded them to live a good life, for 'as we are now so shall you be'.

This sculpture in St Peter's Ketteringham, from the latter part of the seventeenth century, shows the lingering influence of kneeler monuments. The angel flying across the black tablet carries away a chrysom child in its swaddling cloth, sowing confusion in the minds of those trying to read the inscription. You will search in vain for Sir William Heveningham's name, it doesn't appear here nor on his tomb slab on the floor. Sir William was one of the judges at King Charles I's trial. He didn't sign the death warrant but, after the Restoration, was convicted of high treason and his lands seized by the Crown. His life was spared and through the exertions of his wife – Lady Mary Heveningham, daughter of the Earl of Dover – the estate was recovered. In 1678 she erected this family curiously old-fashioned memorial but her husband's name is absent.

Saints Peter and Paul, Heydon

The Heveningham memorial, 1678, St Peter's Ketteringham

In the 1700s, tomb-chests became far less common and were replaced by wall monuments and tablets that were more restrained in spirit. Elements of Classicism, already established in the previous century, came to the fore. To put the period into local historical perspective, this was when Holkham Hall was being built in the Palladian style – a purer vision of Classical than the theatrical Baroque. One of the outstanding London sculptors of the age, Frenchman Louis François Roubiliac (1702-1762), was never commissioned to build a tomb in Norfolk although he did sculpt the busts of Lord Leicester, Thomas Coke (d. 1759), and his wife on their monument in Tittleshall. Adjacent to this

is a piece by the fashionable London sculptor Joseph Nollekens (d. 1823). Though he was said to have been to sculpture what Sir Joshua Reynolds was to portraiture (i.e., fashionable and prolific) Nollekens only sculpted two pieces in Norfolk, one of them being the bas relief of 1805 to Jane Coke, wife of the great agriculturalist, 'Coke of Norfolk'. The broken column on which she rests symbolises her early death aged 47.

The Hare Mausoleum, built in 1624 by John Hare on the north side of the chancel of Holy Trinity Stow Bardolph, houses the most curious memorial in the county. This is the wax effigy of Sarah Hare in her mahogany case, emerging from behind curtains, as directed in her will. She is thought to have died in 1774 of blood poisoning after pricking her finger while embroidering and it was her wish to be remembered in her everyday clothes. The

Jane Coke's memorial by Nollekens. Her bust by Roubiliac is to the left

Sarah Hare d.1744. Holy Trinity, Stow Bardolph

model is unflattering and the effect of her gaze has been described as 'shattering' and 'terrifying' – an antidote to sentimental memorials that dissembled the reality of death.

Norwich mayors were elected annually. In life, their parish churches would have celebrated by adding their name plaque to ceremonial sword and mace rests, usually attached to a pillar. Norwich probably has more of these sword rests than anywhere outside London. In death, a memorial to the mayor would have been placed on a wall. Here, in St George Colegate, Philip Meadows (mayor in 1734) and John Hall (1701&1719) are remembered by their mural monuments of stone and by the metal name-plaques on the nearby sword rest. Norwich had more than a score of sculptors who could produce the increasingly popular wall tablets equal to the best work from London. The leading

Nathaniel Mickelthwait by Robert Page 1757

Memorials to mayors Philip Meadows and John Hall in St George's, Colegate

'Norwich School' sculptors included Robert Page (1707-1778), Thomas Rawlins (1747-1781) and Robert Singleton (1706-1740). Singleton came from Bury St Edmunds although his workshop was adjacent to Norwich Cathedral where Robert Page served his apprenticeship.

Hovering around the top tier of Norwich monumental masons was John Ivory (1730-1805/6) whose wall monument carved for his uncle, the architect Thomas Ivory, we saw at the end of the previous chapter. John took over Page's shop and yard at the corner of King Street and Tombland, just outside the cathedral's Ethelbert Gate. Now the site of the All Bar One restaurant, this was near the site of the Popinjay Inn, the origin of the great fire of 1507 that burned 718 buildings.

Singleton's pupil, Page, has been considered the best sculptor that Norfolk has produced. His work is characterised by the use of colourful marble veneers and 'delightful' cherubs as illustrated by this wall monument in Saints Mary and Margaret, Sprowston.

Sarcophagus end by Robert Page 1751, at St Peter's, Ketteringham

Churchman's name can be found on a mayoral sword rest inside the church as can the wall monument marking his death in 1747, the latter being the only recorded example in the county by London's Sir Henry Cheere. The use of mournful cherubs' heads in the panel at the bottom of the tablet was a common device – an echo, perhaps, of kneeling weepers. Cherubs were ubiquitous in this period – churches and graveyards positively thrum with them. Perhaps they satisfied the need for a figurative presence on often quite plain tablets, adding a touch of humanity to a slab of cold marble. Norwich sculptors employed this trope and here is the work of John Ivory compared with the work of Westminster Abbey's 'carver', Cheere.

Page was also known for carving handsome sarcophagi; a particularly fine example with detailed lions' feet memorialises Edward Atkyns (d.1750), Lord of the Manor at Ketteringham. The end of a sarcophagus projects part way out of the wall, showing how the narrow end of a sarcophagus or casket came to provide the format – lozenge or rectangle – for less florid wall tablets.

A later lord of the manor with the same name, Edward Atkyns (d.1794), scandalised the county by marrying an Irish actress, Charlotte Walpole, who performed at Drury Lane. Shunned by the local squirearchy, they moved to France where she became friends with Marie Antoinette and is said to have squandered the family's money in plots to release the queen and her son, Louis XVII, from prison. In one account Charlotte – reprising her performance at Drury Lane – dressed as a soldier of the National Guard in order to release the unfortunate queen. The romantic story of her escapades in Paris appears in the book 'Mrs Pimpernel Atkyns' by EEP Tisdall.

Sir Thomas Churchman's fine house on St Giles Plain lies equidistant between his triangular walk in Chapelfield Gardens and Great St Giles Church.

Cherubs compared. Top, by Sir Henry Cheere, St Giles', Norwich; bottom, by John Ivory, St Stephen's, Norwich. Both 1747.

The Classical influences that dominated the Regency period lingered until the time of Queen Victoria's accession (1837) after which, according to some, there was an aesthetic decline. John Flaxman (1775-1826) was one of the most famous artists of the early nineteenth century and representative of this pre-Victorian

Memorial for Harriot Peach by John Flaxman at St Peter's, Ketteringham

Memorial to circus proprietor John Barker d.1897. Rosary Cemetery, Norwich.

period. For the memorial to Harriot Peach (d.1825) at Ketteringham he used a favourite motif of a young woman being borne to heaven by two angels. It is undeniably sentimental yet the whole effect is restrained and elegant as might be expected of the man who began his career by modelling neo-classical reliefs to be applied to Josiah Wedgwood's pottery.

From its inception in the 1830s, the Anglo-Catholic Oxford Movement raised ideological objections to large and boastful monuments, creating the climate for a countrywide proliferation of plain wall tablets, but hardly anything bigger. Classical design was considered pagan so religious buildings were to be in the Gothic style and certainly no later than Decorated. In Norwich,

local tradition influenced the celebration of death. Throughout the eighteenth and nineteenth centuries the city's population contained a high percentage of Dissenters. An Act of 1836 allowed Nonconformists to perform their own funeral services but it was not until 1880 that they were allowed to conduct burials in parish churches according to their own rites. However, in 1819, Thomas Drummond had established the Rosary Cemetery in the Norwich suburb of Thorpe Hamlet – the first in the country where anyone could be buried regardless of their religion. As a result, the monuments in The Rosary are gloriously various, from the plainness of Quaker memorials to some that would have been on the Oxford Movement's proscribed list.

In 1775, Reverend James Woodforde came to Weston Longville, a small village north of Norwich where he remained as rector until his death in 1803. During this time he kept a diary of his life as a country parson but city-dwellers will find it intriguing for his glimpses into late eighteenth century Norwich.

James Woodforde from a sketch (1785), by his nephew Samuel Woodforde RA (1806).
Credit: Parson Woodforde Society.

Norwich has changed a good deal across the two hundred and fifty or so years between Parson Woodforde's time and ours. The Industrial Revolution, World War II bombing raids, slum clearance, a new City Hall, and reconfiguring a medieval city around the motor car, have all left their mark. Still, some of the Norwich known to Woodforde glimmers through. In his journal, published as The Diary of a Country Parson 1758-1802, Woodforde recorded his thoughts about neighbours, servants, gargantuan meat-rich suppers and his frequent visits to Norwich for diversion. We start at the marketplace and won't stray far.

The present market, which was established by the Normans, supplanted the Anglo-Scandinavian trading place in Tombland to become the thriving hub of the city for almost a thousand years. Here it is in John Sell Cotman's 'Norwich Market-Place' (1809), not long after Woodforde's death. Overlooking all is the tower of St Peter Mancroft.

Although the multi-paned shop windows of the Georgian era have been replaced by sheets of plate glass, which started to appear towards the end of Victoria's reign, Gentleman's Walk to the left would still be recognisable to the parson. As a member of highly stratified Georgian society – on the lower end, admittedly, but a member nonetheless – Woodforde would have mixed with the gentlefolk promenading along the fashionable Walk but his shopping trips would also have taken him amongst the working folk in the market itself.

The fronts of these buildings along the east side of the marketplace were separated from the Norman Great Market by what appears on Samuel King's plan of 1766 as 'Nether Row or Gentleman's Walk'. 'Nether' refers to a lower row of market stalls arranged outside the inns but as early as 1681 Thomas Baskerville had written about 'a fair walk before the prime inns and

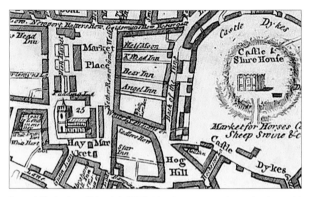

Samuel King's plan of Norwich (1766). Four inns connect the marketplace with The Back of the Inns. Photo: author, courtesy of Norwich County Council.

Norwich Market-Place by JS Cotman (1809). Public domain..

houses of the market-place… called gentlemen's walk or walking place… kept clear for the purposes from the encumbrances of stalls, tradesman and their goods'. Evidently, the walkway outside the inns had become an acceptable place for members of an increasingly polite and enlightened society to promenade, separated from the hurly-burly of the market.

King's map shows the lane running behind and parallel to Gentleman's Walk as Back of the Inns, a service road connecting the outbuildings of The Half Moon Inn, The King's Head Inn, The Bear Inn and The Angel Inn. Parson Woodforde drank coffee at The Angel but he preferred to lodge at The King's Head. It was from here that the Norwich mail coach departed for Yarmouth. From 1802, two mail coaches left here daily for London ('the London machine'): one via Ipswich and one via Newmarket. Cotman has depicted some of these coaches further along Gentleman's Walk.

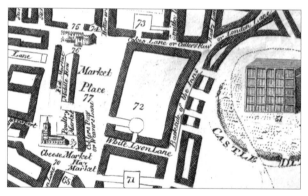

Francis Blomefield's plan of Norwich 1746.
Photo: author, courtesy of Norfolk Record Office

Inns ringed the marketplace and the amount of stabling required by the four on the east side alone must have been considerable. Perhaps Francis Blomefield on his map of 1746 was simply echoing local humour when he labelled this lane, Backside of the Inns.

In 1775, Woodforde journeyed from London to Norwich by post chaise and four: '109 miles, and the best of roads I have ever travelled.' Arriving after ten o'clock at night he found the city gates – presumably St Stephen's Gate – shut, reminding us that the medieval defences were still largely intact at that time. At the end of the century the gates would be pulled down and the stretch of city wall to the north of St Stephen's Gate used as hardcore for the new Prince of Wales Road. Built in the 1860s, this was intended as a grand approach to connect the new Thorpe railway station with the city centre.

Small changes to the marketplace accrued after Woodforde died. In 1840, when Queen Victoria married, the fifteenth century Angel Inn was patriotically renamed The Royal. In 1899 it would be demolished and replaced with a fashionable arcade designed by George Skipper, architect of the city's 'fireworks'. Moulded in marble-like Carrara Ware by Doulton's WJ Neatby, the winged figure above the Back of the Inns entrance commemorates the original Angel Inn. As the Royal Inn was disappearing (1896-7), Edward Boardman was building a new Royal Hotel on Agricultural Hall Plain, larger and closer to the railway station.

Angel at the east end of Royal Arcade, on Back of the Inns

Norwich Castle and Gentleman's Walk'. Lithograph by J Newman (1850).
Courtesy of David Clarke.

Newman's lithograph of 1850 provides a sense of the fashionable stores along the east side of the marketplace – an early shopping parade. Woodforde is known to have visited John Toll's draper's shop in the marketplace. He paid seven shillings and sixpence for a pair of cotton stockings for his niece Anna Maria (Nancy) who was his housekeeper and companion. At the shop of Mr Tandy (a 'Chymist and a Druggist') he spent three shillings on an ounce of 'Rhubarb', presumably tincture of rhubarb taken for digestive complaints. For thruppence he also purchased Goulard's Extract, used for inflammation of the skin, although this was later discontinued as it was found to cause lead poisoning.

In Woodforde's time there was no wide street exiting the square at the north-east corner where Jarrold's department store now stands. But in 1832 Exchange Street was cut through, connecting the market to St Andrew's Street and over the newly erected Duke's Palace Bridge towards North Norfolk.

In 1812, Alderman Jonathan Davey – Baptist Radical of Eaton Hall – announced in a council meeting that

he would put a hole in the king's head. What he really meant was that Gentleman's Walk would be breached after he had bought and demolished The King's Head Hotel but his joke misfired and his seditious words led to a guard being placed upon his house for his own safety. Having pulled down Woodforde's preferred coaching inn, the alderman built a shop-lined thoroughfare that connected the livestock markets around the castle with the marketplace. Exchange Street and Davey Place belong to a small group of post-medieval Norwich streets.

In Woodforde's time the Castle would have been ringed by various markets, each dedicated to the sale of particular livestock. The 'Davey Steps' connecting Davey Place to Castle Meadow provided a barrier to

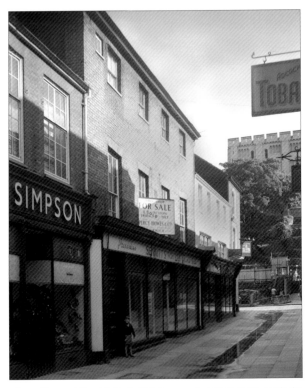
Davey Place and Norwich Castle 1961. ©georgeplunkett.co.uk. The boy in the shadows is Jonathan, son of the photographer.

Demolition of municipal buildings at back of the market 1938
© georgeplunkett.co.uk

As the Back of the Inns followed the curve of Castle Meadow it flowed into medieval London Lane. This route was narrow and far from ideal and there are reports of pedestrians sheltering in doorways from wagons. In 1844 the opening of Norwich railway station (later, Norwich Thorpe) created demand for better access to and from the market, as a result of which London Street was widened. To achieve this, most of the medieval buildings familiar to Woodforde were demolished. He would, though, have known this grand doorway from the house of John Bassingham, a goldsmith from Henry VIII's time, now inserted into the magistrate's entrance of the Guildhall.

animals, although not an insurmountable one. Mackie's Norfolk Annals reported that in April 1823: 'A man who sold sand about the streets of Norwich drove his cart and pair of horses up the flight of ten steps, leading from Davey Place to the Castle ditches. The horses did it with much ease and without receiving any injury, to the astonishment of the spectators'.

In the Fish Market at the back of the marketplace, Woodforde bought soles from Mr Beale, which were sometimes less than fresh. In the days before refrigeration he would also take home oysters from the market; sometimes he bought them from 'an old man of Reepham'. The insanitary fish market was replaced in 1860 by a Neoclassical building at the Guildhall Hill end of St Peters Street. In 1938 this structure was pulled down to make way for the Memorial Gardens as part of the new City Hall scheme. By this time the fish market had moved to Mountergate (1914-1980) where its former presence is marked by a plaque on the side of the Rose Lane car park. Other buildings demolished at the back of the marketplace included the Tin Hut – used as police station and drill hall – and more substantial Municipal Buildings.

The Bassingham doorway installed in the Guildhall

Woodforde's ambit does seem limited for much of his business for much of his business could be conducted within hailing distance of the marketside inns. Edward Freeman's premises were in the Back of the Inns. Freeman made high quality picture frames and rococo furniture for country houses like Felbrigg Hall and Blickling Hall. The diaries tell us that Parson Woodforde bought furniture from him but only the everyday kind, paying a guinea deposit for two mahogany chests of drawers and half a dozen ash kitchen chairs.

Edward Freeman's frame for Amelia Opie's medallion. Courtesy of Norwich School.

Just around the corner, Woodforde visited his upholsterer, James Sudbury in Cockey Lane at the Guildhall end of London Street. In 1793, two of Sudbury's workmen, Abraham Seely and Isaac Warren, claimed to have carried a 'large New Mohogany Cellarett' and a sideboard 'on the Men's shoulders all the way'; that is, nine miles to Weston Longville. For this Herculean feat Woodforde fed and watered the men and gave

them a shilling tip but one can't help wondering if the upholsterer's cart was hidden down the lane.

Woodforde also acted as a financial go-between for his friend Henry Bathurst, later to become the Bishop of Norwich and have a street in the Golden Triangle named after him. Bathurst was non-resident parson of a neighbouring parish so had tithes collected on his behalf. In order to send the money to his friend in Oxford, Parson Woodforde would exchange bills and cash for a banknote at Kerrison's Norwich Bank, in the Back of the Inns. On one occasion Woodforde sent a note for £137 by post to his friend in Oxford then celebrated his good deed by dining at the King's Head on a mutton chop and a bottle of wine. Five years after Woodforde's death, Sir Roger Kerrison was to die in an apoplectic fit after which his bank failed, unable to pay the Government the money he had collected as Receiver-General

In 1793, Parson Woodforde banked £2-12s-0d, collected at Weston Longville for emigré French clergy. These refugees from the French Revolution joined a succession of French Protestants who had been finding sanctuary here since the sixteenth century. Not far from the main market was the smaller Hay Market (and Cheese Market) where Woodforde had his watchspring repaired by master watch-maker Peter Amyot, a descendant of French Huguenots. In his diary, the parson also mentions other descendants of immigrants: like James Rump, grocer and tallow chandler (whose name had been anglicised from Rumpf); Elisha de Hague, attorney; and the influential Martineau family, underlining the contribution that newcomers made to this city's commerce.

PARSON WOODFORDE
AND THE LEARNED PIG

We don't read The Diary of a Country Parson for the grand sweep of history but for the finer grain of his daily life. Parson Woodforde's diaries are history slowed. We hear in detail what ails his parishioners and of his small kindnesses but we are left to infer the causes of rural poverty for ourselves. When the American War of Independence depressed the export of Norwich textiles in 1781 Woodforde noted laconically, 'Trade at Norwich never worse. Poor no employment.' James Woodforde occupied the still centre while history crashed around him. He was, however, more forthcoming about the minutiae of his comfortable living as vicar of Weston Longville. From the ten-mile excursions he took into Norwich we learn about the texture of life in a provincial Georgian city.

In April 1775, when Parson Woodforde and his companions had to rouse the gatekeeper to let them through St Stephens Gate, they spent the night at the King's Head in the marketplace. For their journey from London they had arisen early and hired a post chaise and four through Epping Forest. This was not without peril for this is where a coachman was killed by a gang of seven highwaymen after shooting three of them. Woodforde's party changed coach and horses at 'The Bull-Faced Stagg' then proceeded to Harlow; onwards to Stanstead, then to Bourne Bridge with fresh chaises to Newmarket where they dined. In fresh chaises they drove to Barton Mills (where they changed yet again) and on to Thetford, Attleborough and Norwich. The details emphasise the effort and expense to get from the

St Stephens Gate by John Moray-Smith, displayed on the nearby Coachmakers Arms. Public domain

capital to what had been the nation's second city; more byzantine even than the replacement bus service faced by rail commuters between Norwich and Liverpool Street. This journey by coach cost Woodforde's party eleven pounds, fourteen shillings and fourpence, of which the parson paid half – more than he would pay a young servant maid per annum.

The slowness of travel made villages more isolated than they are today. Before the standardising effects of railway timetables, communities were necessarily more self-sustaining to the extent that cities across the country kept their own times. Woodforde evidently required more than Weston Longville could offer and was willing to drive his horse and cart the ten miles to Norwich. In 1791, he replaced his 'old little cart' with 'a new little Curricle painted a deep Green and without Springs - 9 guineas' ... like it much.' He had bought this light two-wheeled cart from Adams and Bacon of 3 St Stephens Road whose premises were near the St Stephens Gate that had once barred him from entering the city. The gate was demolished in 1793 but the nearby Coachmakers Arms survives.

When he travelled from Weston Longville to Norwich, Woodforde stabled his horse in St Giles Street, at the Woolpack, later to become the Norfolk Hotel. In 1904 it

The Norfolk Hotel, St Giles Street, Norwich. Late C19. Courtesy of Norfolk County Council Library and Information Service

would be demolished to make way for the Grand Opera House, which then became a theatre and cinema – The Hippodrome. In World War II, the theatre took a direct hit from a German bomb, killing the theatre manager, his wife and a sea lion trainer. From 1966, the site was to become the St Giles car park.

Etching of JF Priest Chymist and Druggist (1825-50) by his son Alfred Priest.
Credit: The Trustees of the British Museum

The hotel on St Giles Street was only a few yards from a wine shop and druggists where Woodforde was a frequent visitor. Peck's Norwich Directory of 1802 gives this as 'Priest, John Fox, Chymist and Druggist, 1, St. Giles' Broad Str'. When in the city, the parson would call in for tea or dine with the Priest family (when 'dining' meant a meal at 3pm). Once he stayed after election night and on another occasion paid for John Priest's theatre ticket. The parson was a good customer of Priests's wine business where, in preparation for the arrival of his relatives from Somerset, Woodforde, 'tasted some Wine and ordered a Quarter of a Pipe [a pipe of port is 60 gallons], -with 3 gallons of Rum and 3 gallons of the best Holland Geneva [gin]'. These are, quite literally, staggering quantities but then Woodforde would drink a pint of port with a meal.

Bishop Bathurst (1744-1837) in Norwich Cathedral

*Tithes represented one tenth of the produce raised on church-owned land. Originally, the monetary equivalent was paid to the Pope but when Henry VIII became head of the Church of England he fixed the cash value of tithes. When the Crown sold church land to secular institutions the tithes came with it. After 1836, tithes became replaced with the tithe rent charge. Oxford and Cambridge colleges owned about 5% of livings, which they were free to award to their fellows.

It is not surprising, therefore, that the first Norwich house Woodforde visited after arriving in Norfolk in 1776 was Number Three Surrey Street. This was the address of Robert Francis and Son, attorneys, who administered New College's Norfolk livings, and where Woodforde 'called on Mr Francis Junr and talked with him a good deal.' Surrey Street is a fine Georgian thoroughfare, part of which was designed by the architect of Georgian Norwich, Thomas Ivory. The street was badly damaged by the Baedeker Raids of 1942 and by insensitive twentieth century additions (making an exception for George Skipper's Marble Hall for Norwich Union). We must thank George Plunkett for recording Number Three in 1936.

How could a cleric live so well? We already know that Woodforde collected tithes* for his Oxford friend Henry Bathurst; these were received from Great Witchingham, a parish three miles from his own. The diary records that when he was at Oxford in 1775, Woodforde himself received a Norwich Bank bill from his curate for £150, 'being part of money for Tithes* received for me at Weston.' In 1777, on his 'Frolic Day', when he received two hundred and four pounds and seventeen shillings for 'tithe and glebe', he entertained about 20 of his parishioners and fed and watered them handsomely. The Church – or more specifically the living from the parish of All Saints, Weston Longville – afforded James Woodforde the life of a gentleman and a respectable position in a hierarchical society.

Number 3 Surrey Street in 1936 (no longer extant) ©georgeplunkett.co.uk

After the religious upheavals of earlier centuries the late 1700s were a time of relative stability; Norwich emerged into an Age of Reason in which polite society with time to spare would meet in coffee houses, window-shop along Gentleman's Walk and promenade in Chapelfield Gardens. There was theatre, public lectures, pleasure gardens, subscription to an increasing number of libraries and – the gravitational centre for the city's fashionable – assemblies held at Chapelfield House, recently renovated by Thomas Ivory. It would probably have been unseemly for the parson to attend public dances but in the evening of December 1785, Woodforde visited the Assembly House to see an 'excellent lecture on Astronomy etc.'. This may have been delivered by Adam Walker – a well-known scholar whose lectures at Syon House Academy and Eton had instilled in the poet Shelley a love of science. To further enlighten Norwich on the motions of the planets, Walker (or perhaps his son William) was aided by his eidouranion – a large mechanical orrery, some fifteen feet square, that seems to have been back-projected onto a screen. The device

was still in service in the early nineteenth century when one of Walker's sons, Deane Franklin Walker, carried on the family tradition.

Walker's lectures on planetary motion inspired Romantics with a sense of the sublime – that they were part of something greater. Woodforde's terse comment was that he 'was highly pleased with it', but beneath his anodyne words darker forces ran. The toleration of Nonconformity and the rise of Evangelism – all quite alien to an Anglican parson – had created a climate of intellectual and political dissent such that Norwich was described as a Jacobin city by Prime Minister William Pitt City. Republicanism was in the air and Amelia Opie, the epitome of the city's radical spirit, went to see the results of the French Revolution for herself.

Parson Woodforde's diary is not completely silent about the mob. On the evening of June 9th 1778 he witnessed 'a great Riot upon the Castle Hill between the officers of the Western Battalion of the Norfolk Militia and the common soldiers and Mob.' The officers had refused to pay the men a guinea each, as a consequence of which some of the soldiers had refused to take up arms and were put into the guard room. When the mob insisted on hauling them out a great riot ensued. The mob threw stones, some were wounded by bayonets but no-one was killed.

Walker's eidouranion at the English Opera House in The Strand, 1817.
Public domain

Norfolk Militia practicing musketry 1759. Public domain

Circling back to St Stephens Gate, Woodforde's port of entry to the city, we know that the parson visited a pleasure garden on what is now the south-west side of the roundabout. Before Marsh Insurance, and before that the Victoria railway station, the site was occupied by Quantrell's pleasure gardens, which the parson helps brings alive:

> near 6 o'clock ...walked to Quantrells Gardens by myself, heard a sad Concert and saw the Fireworks which were very good and worth seeing gave on going [one shilling] for which you have 6d worth of anything at the Bar. I supped and spent the evening there and stayed till 12 o'clock. For my Supper and Liquor pd [one shilling and sixpence] A very heavy Storm fell about 9 o'clock. A prodigious number of common girls [i.e., prostitutes] there and dressed. The Fire Works began about 11 o'clock and lasted about an hour. In it, a representation of the Engagement between the English and French Fleet under Sir George Rodney. (Woodforde's diary, June 20 1780).

The owner, Quantrell, was originally employed as a fireworks engineer so the pyrotechnics are likely to have been spectacular. This was part of the competition between the city's various pleasure gardens that tried to ape the post-Restoration venues in London. Quantrell's Gardens were at one time named Ranelagh Gardens after the London attraction. In Thackeray's novel, Vanity Fair, Becky Sharpe visited the capital's fashionable Vauxhall Gardens; Norwich was to have its own Vauxhall when the New Spring Gardens behind King Street were renamed at the end of the eighteenth century.

It was at the New Spring Gardens that Parson Woodforde saw the Sons of Neptune go down the river by boat, accompanied by a very good band. But it was back in Quantrell's that he saw Mr Decker (also Deeker) and Major Money ascend in their lighter-than-air balloons, for this was the age of Balloon Mania. John

Major Money adrift in the North Sea. Credit: The Metropolitan Museum of Art

Money, whose military career had started in the Norfolk Militia, was an intrepid local aeronaut and when he ascended he went almost over Woodforde's head as he stood in Bracondale. This was some seven weeks before the major's balloon famously deposited him in the sea off Yarmouth for several hours.

Other amusements mentioned in the diary include the 'Man Satire' (satyr) that the parson saw on Castle Hill with his friends, the two Priests. Having laid out sixpence he was most disappointed: it 'was nothing more than a large Monkey ... It did not answer our Expectations at all.' He was, however, 'highly Astonished' with the life-size wax doll on show in St Stephens since the automaton could answer, and pose, questions. But the highlight is to be found in the entry for December 19th 1785. This was the day the parson attended Walker's lecture on astronomy in the evening but earlier that day he 'went and saw the learned Pigg at the rampant Horse in St Stephens.' In bracketing the sublime and the wonderfully ridiculous, Woodforde's day illustrates the uncritical nature of public spectacle

The Learned Pig paperweight with fridge magnets

in the Age of Enlightenment. Historian Angela Dain summed this up as: 'the desire for mystery rather than elucidation, and the accompanying perception of science and technology as magical rather than empirical disciplines'.

There have been many clever pigs but this animal, 'Toby, The Amazing Pig of Knowledge', was the one trained by Samuel Bissett. After Bissett died as a result of being assaulted by a man with a sword, Toby was bought by a Mr Nicholson who brought him to Norwich. The 'rampant Horse in St Stephens', where the Pigg performed, was a large medieval coaching inn that would disappear to make way for the Curl Brothers' department store (itself bombed and replaced by Debenhams) on what is now Rampant Horse Street. For

his shilling, Woodforde saw the animal 'with a magic Collar on his Neck. He would spell any Number from the Letters and Figures that were placed before him.' Advertisements claimed Toby was capable of much more than typographical tricks: he could reckon the number of people present, tell the hours and minutes of a watch, distinguish between the married and unmarried and divine any Lady's Thoughts.

The Learned Pig achieved national fame. It was mentioned inWordsworth's Prelude (1805): 'The horse of knowledge, and the learned pig'. And the poet Southey went so far as to say that the pig was, 'a far greater object of admiration for the British nation than ever was Sir Isaac Newton.'

In the late eighteenth century, voting by the Norwich freemen for sheriff, mayor and aldermen was highly factional and often violent. Anti-Establishment feeling was also roused amongst the high proportion of Dissenters who wished to preserve their religious freedoms.

Such was the radicalism that the Prime Minister called Norwich the Jacobin city, alluding to the extreme French revolutionaries. The fear was that this could, as in America and France, tip over into Revolution. Delacroix's painting does not, as one correspondent asked, show St Peter Mancroft Norwich in the background.

As a rich and loyal city, Norwich had been awarded a degree of political independence by the monarchy. In 1194, Richard the Lionheart allowed the royal lion to be shown on the city's coat of arms – a sign that marked the city's right to elect its own Reeve. In 1404 Henry IV increased the number of MPs from two to four and granted the city the special status of a county (The County of the City of Norwich) governed by a sheriff; this lasted until the local government reforms of 1974. These freedoms meant that civic matters could be decided in a common assembly composed of freemen, i.e., men whose fathers had been freemen, or who had been apprenticed to a freeman for seven years, or who purchased the right.

Liberty leading the People, by Eugène Delacroix. Credit: The Louvre, Paris.

Chairing the Members. Plate IV, by William Hogarth, 1758. Public domain

At a time when few common men had the right to vote, these historic privileges paved the way for the violent political groupings that had evolved in the years after Henry VIII broke the relationship between Church and Crown. Historian Mark Knights commented, that by 1681 the city was polarised between 'two factions, the Whigs and the Tories, and both contend for their way with the utmost violence'. In the late eighteenth century the Whigs rallied under the Blue and Buff (or Blue and White) flag, and Tories wore Purple and Orange. To oversimplify their differences, the Whigs were originally liberal parliamentarians opposed to the absolute monarchy offered by the Catholic James II, while the conservative Tories were for high church and the Crown.

Compared to other large cities, such as Exeter and Bristol, Norwich would appear to have enjoyed a remarkably open and popular civic structure. In 1790 there were 2480 electors who could vote three times a year for the mayor, the sheriff and the common council. In addition, Norwich freeholders could vote for two MPs. The frequency of elections ensured the political pot never went off the boil, perhaps explaining the reports of post-election fights, leading on occasion to the reading of the Riot Act.

Triumphal arch in Norwich marketplace, by Paul Fourdrinier 1746.
Courtesy of David Clarke.

After the Catholic monarch, James II, attempted to impose absolute rule on the country he was resisted by the Glorious Revolution of 1688 in which he was displaced, bloodlessly, by the Protestant William of Orange and his wife Mary II. From this time, Norwich Tory sentiment was tinged with Jacobitism – support for the restoration of the Catholic House of Stuart (Jacobus = James). During the Jacobite Rebellion of 1745-6, Charles Edward Stuart's army crossed the border, invading as far as Derby. When the Duke of Cumberland defeated the Jacobites at Culloden the Norwich Whigs celebrated with an extravagant feast and erected a triumphal arch in the marketplace. The structure was covered in 96 yards of Persian silk, painted with motifs and slogans such as 'Religion' and 'Liberty'. These would be illuminated at night 'with many hundred lights placed within.'

'Liberty', code for political and religious independence, was the watchword for the Whigs. In 1768, Sir Thomas Beevor (1726-1814) of Hethel Hall stood as a Whig candidate in the Norwich parliamentary election, promising to fight against *'all attempts upon the liberty of the Subject and every other unconstitutional measure'*. He was unsuccessful then and again in 1786 and 1790. To stifle Beevor's independence, the sitting MP – Harbord Harbord, 1st Lord Suffield of Gunton Hall – was asked to join forces, or make a 'junction' with, another candidate, Edmund Bacon. Five hundred Norwich freemen cried out against this chicanery. In a satirical print by an unknown artist, the Norwich crowd cries out for Beevor while, inside, a red-coated Harbord Harbord is being pressed to support a porcine Edmund Bacon.

Having only just subdued its own rebellion, England in the last quarter of the eighteenth century was unsettled by revolution on three sides: the American War of Independence (1775-1783), the French Revolution (1789-1794) and the Irish Rebellion of 1798. Unsurprisingly, Norwich politics split along party lines. A certain ambivalence, however, was reflected in the career of the city's most eminent politician of the period, William Windham (1750-1810), who was member of parliament for Norwich from 1789-1802. The son of William Windham Senior of Felbrigg Hall in North Norfolk, Windham Jr was intellectually gifted, eloquent and charming … but chronically indecisive. When, in 1792, Windham supported the Ministry in calling out the militia he was voting for measures of which he had previously disapproved. A satirical cartoon

'The Junction', artist unknown. Wikimedia Commons.

by Cruikshank portrays the MP as Weathercock Windham. He stands on a rotating platform while declaiming, "Down with the Volunteers !! ... They are all Democrats!" And the common man says, "Why Master Whirligig ... now you want us not to fight that Butcher Boneyparte...".

Windham was an enemy of the slave trade and should have been a favourite of Norwich's intellectual left, which included abolitionists like Elizabeth Fry and Amelia Opie. However, his contradictory views on reform and his opposition to peace with France alienated the city's Whigs. In 1794, this one-time Blue and White executed an about-turn when he became war minister on an Orange and Purple ticket. Two years later, Parson Woodforde wrote, 'Mr Wyndham very unpopular at present amongst the Revolutionists and which are great numbers at Norwich, especially Dissenters. Knuckle of Veal and boiled tongue for dinner to day.'

Amelia Opie in her high Quaker bonnet, with a display of anti-slavery material in Norwich Castle Museum

This quotation from Woodforde reveals a separate strand of anti-Establishment feeling that can be traced to religious nonconformity, which had been strong in Norwich since the late seventeenth century. The Act of Uniformity (1662) aimed to suppress dissent by requiring ministers to observe the rites and sacraments of the Established Church of England or be ejected for their nonconformity. In 1689, the Act of Toleration allowed Protestant nonconformists to have their own places of worship on condition they made certain oaths of allegiance. The beautiful Old Meeting House in Colegate was one of the first such tolerated places (1693).

The Old Meeting House, Colegate. 1693

Politics and religious freedom were tightly interwoven, making it inevitable that dissenters would have to enter the political sphere if they were to protect their religious independence. The Norwich Quakers were prominent dissenters and John Gurney, father of Elizabeth Fry and partner in Gurney's Bank (precursor to Barclay's Bank), is said to have bankrolled the Norwich Blue and Whites. It is estimated that one seventh of the Norwich population were Protestant dissenters at the beginning of the 1700s. And in the mid-1700s half of the serving mayors came from nonconformist backgrounds. Dissent was endemic in the wards either side of the River Wensum: Wymer and Norwich-over-the-Water. These wards were in the heart of the city's textile industry where Jeremiah Ives and Thomas and Robert Harvey

CATTON HALL, NORFOLK.

Catton Hall and Park in 1856. Courtesy of David Clarke.

– mayors made rich by the wool trade – were based. In addition to their town houses on Colegate all three were a short carriage ride away from their country estates just north of the city. After Thomas Ives moved into Catton Hall in the late 1780s he engaged the leading landscape architect, Humphry Repton, to redesign the park from which he could see Norwich in the distance.

As a Whig mayor, Ives kept a paternalistic eye on his supporters. In return for helping their cause, the city's yarn makers sponsored a full length portrait. When he was elected mayor for the second time the parishioners of St Clement erected a triumphal arch over the street at his townhouse at number 1 Colegate. The Harvey

family were also known for their support of the weavers and for the distress of the poor. Like Ives, second-time mayor Robert Harvey was the recipient of a triumphal arch covered in evergreens and draped with flowers, its battlements concealing a music gallery. But Harvey behaved less heroically to his religious neighbours who worshipped in Thomas Ivory's Octagon Chapel across the road in Colegate; in a political handbill he complained about the 'duplicity of the Quakers and the cant of the Presbyterians'. Countering this, Edward Crane, son of a Unitarian minister and himself a preacher at the Octagon Chapel, said that the city had for a long time been slave to the Ives and the Harveys who nominated all the members of the city corporation

The Bell Inn on Orford Hill, 1936. Originally named The Blue Bell Inn 1743-1822. ©georgeplunkett.co.uk

French Revolution he gave a sermon on *'The origin and stability of the French Revolution'*, quoting from the bible, 'If it be of God ye cannot overthrow it' (Acts V, 39).

John Harvey, the Tory mayor in 1792, was notable for introducing what was to become the famous Norwich shawl at a time when the city's textile industry was in a major recession. That year, at a dinner in the King's Head, he toasted: 'May the seeds of sedition never take root in British soil. May Pain (Thetford-born Thomas Paine who had just published *'Rights of Man'*) be expelled from every British bosom'. A week later, Harvey dined at The Maid's Head where he referred to those who '... meant to delude and ensnare the lower classes of the people, from whose labours our manufactures thrive and commerce flourishes'. Evidently, men of business feared the effects of seditious propaganda upon their workers.

despite the fact that the city's freemen were entitled by charter to vote in the common assembly.

This one Norwich street illustrates the struggle between the free church and the rich master weavers for the hearts – or votes – of the working freemen weavers. Conversely, it shows the efforts made by the weavers to mollify their bosses, even though they may have disagreed with their politics. The Loyal Society of Worsted Weavers, for example, were so staunchly Whig that they would throw out any member who voted Tory.

Towards the end of that century, the Revolution Society was formed, purportedly to celebrate the centenary of the Glorious Revolution of 1688 but it was likely that its founders were keeping a watchful eye on events that would soon lead to the French Revolution (1789). The Norwich branch consisted of around 4000 members from forty subsidiary clubs whose delegates met at The Bluebell on Hog Hill (now Orford Hill). The society was based around a nucleus of well-known dissenters including the Baptist minister Mark Wilks – a party worker for the Whigs. He preached that 'Jesus Christ was a revolutionist'. On the second anniversary of the

Rev Mark Wilks ca.1800, by Wm Ridley. Wikimedia Commons

The Whip & Nag pub, formerly The Pelican, in 1956. ©georgeplunkett.co.uk

proved ineffective. At a time when the country was at war with revolutionary France the government regarded a country-wide network of radical societies with the deepest suspicion and, in April 1794, two King's Messengers were sent to Norwich to arrest Isaac Saint. The depth of the Establishment's concern can be judged from the fact that Saint was interrogated next morning by the Privy Council headed by the Lord Chancellor and the Solicitor General. Saint was not sentenced but, with the Habeus Corpus Act suspended, he was 'detained' for two months. The Revolution Society was dissolved soon after.

Harvey would not have had to look far for the source of anti-Tory propaganda. A short walk from Colegate would have taken him to The Pelican public house at the corner of Muspole Street and Pitt Street, which is now the northern end of Duke Street. There he would have found the landlord Isaac Saint, secretary of the Norwich Revolution Society.

In 1793, at a convention held by the Scottish Societies of Friends of the People, it was decided to correspond with all like-minded societies in the kingdom. The Norwich Revolution Society asked London delegate, Maurice Margarot, to represent them. A few months later, when the society had become the British Convention of Friends of the People, its leaders were arrested. Margarot was charged with sedition and transported to Australia for 14 years. While he waited at Spithead for transportation The Norwich Revolution Society sent him £20.

To head off charges of disloyalty, the Norwich Revolution Society declared that class division, riot and disorder played no part in their thinking. The disclaimer

CITIZEN MARGAROT

Delegate from the London Corresponding Society to the British Convention.

Maurice Margarot by John Kay, 1794. Public domain.

I remember watching Sarah Gavron's film, 'Suffragette', in 2015 and experiencing a growing sense of indignation when reading the list of countries that had granted female emancipation long before Great Britain. Women were given the vote as late as 1918, and only then if they were over 30 and owned property. Decades before this, Elizabeth Fry, Amelia Opie and Harriet Martineau – all born into this dissenting city – managed to bring their ideas to national attention.

In a fine example of Norfolk's resentment of injustice (county motto 'Do different'), Wymondham's Robert Kett led 16,000 men in rebellion against the enclosure of land and laid siege to the city. Later, during the Civil War, the city was far from loyal to the monarchy, contributing the 'Maiden Troop' of Ironsides to Cromwell's New Model Army. In the centuries that followed, this sense of independent-mindedness and political radicalism was accompanied by a rise in dissent

Cover of 'The Suffragette' 14-03-1913. National Archives. Open Government Licence.

against the established church. Indeed, by the early eighteenth century, perhaps as many as a fifth of the population were Protestant dissenters. It was into this free-thinking climate that Fry, Opie and Martineau emerged.

Elizabeth Fry (1780-1845) was born in Gurney's Court off Magdalen Street. Her childhood home was not, however, in the huddled weaving streets of Norwich-over-the-water but a few miles outside the city in Earlham Hall, which currently houses the University of East Anglia's School of Law.

Earlham Hall in 1937. ©georgeplunkett.co.uk

Elizabeth came from banking stock. Her mother Catherine was a Barclay; her father John became a partner in Gurneys Bank, founded by a cousin, that would merge in 1896 with other Quaker banks to form Barclays Bank on Bank Plain. Quakers had the reputation for honest dealing and several generations of Gurneys had been financial middle-men in Norwich's textile trade. By the latter quarter of the nineteenth century their fame and wealth were such that one of Gilbert and Sullivan's characters in the opera *Trial by Jury* could be described, 'as rich as the Gurneys'.

In 1800 Elizabeth married John Fry at the Friends' Meeting House in Goat Lane. This was replaced by the new meeting house in 1826, which is the one we see today in Lower Goat Lane – a classically-influenced building with almshouses flanking the small courtyard.

Friends Meeting House 1826, Upper Goat Lane. By Norwich surveyor JT Patience

Elizabeth was greatly influenced by the writing of American Quaker William Savery, leading her to take on the cause of prisoners, the sick and the poor. After moving to London she began to visit women and their children in Newgate Prison where she was appalled by what she saw. This led to her forming the British Ladies' Society for Promoting the Reformation of Women Prisoners, which was the first national women's association in the country. She gave evidence to parliament on prison reform and instigated a training school for nurses that is said to have been the inspiration for Florence Nightingale's mission in the Crimea.

Elizabeth Fry on the back of the £5 note, legal tender until May 2017

By rejecting the authority of the Anglican church in favour of a more personal examination of moral and religious matters, Quakers – like other Dissenters – incurred the displeasure of the establishment. In consequence, Quakers were disbarred from holding certain civil offices and from attending university. The otherness of non-conformists during this period was drawn to my attention when I read an advertisement in The Norwich Mercury (Sat December 2nd 1837) that offered insurance specifically for 'Protestant Dissenters'. They were outsiders. It is therefore remarkable that – as her biographer June Rose said – a dissenting woman, a 'portly matron with ten children ... gatecrashed into public life, into an exclusively male preserve, when the very idea was unthinkable'.

Amelia Opie by her husband John Opie R.A. Public Domain

Amelia Opie (1769-1853) was also born into a Dissenting family, at a house in Colegate, now demolished. Her father James was a physician and her mother (also Amelia) was known locally as a leading proponent of the abolition of slavery. Out of this union emerged a spirited young girl who became a prolific writer of novels, poems and plays; by the age of 18 she had already published (anonymously) a novel entitled *The Dangers of Coquetry*. In her early years Amelia attended the Octagon Chapel along the road from her house, and not far from the town houses of the wealthy master weavers, Ives and the Harveys.

In London, Amelia met the fashionable painter John Opie and they married in 1798 – the year he painted her portrait. In the capital, Amelia was part of a literary circle that included Sir Walter Scott, Wordsworth and Sheridan. During this period she wrote her best known book, the romantic novel *Adeline Mowbray*, which she was encouraged to write by her friend Mary Wollstonecraft – another of John Opie's sitters. Wollstonecraft was famous for having written *A Vindication of the Rights of Woman (1792)* in which she argued that women were not inferior to men, just less well educated. After John Opie's early death in 1807 Amelia returned to live with her father in Norwich where she was encouraged to join the Quakers by Elizabeth Fry and her brother Joseph John Gurney. On becoming a Friend, Amelia stopped writing and in 1825 adopted the clothing of the 'Plain' Quakers. This meant that she shunned the fine clothes that had attracted her as a girl and wore instead drab gowns and plain bonnets. It is in this form of dress that she is depicted on her statue in Opie Street by Norwich sculptor Z Leon (1956). Currently, this artificial stone statue is uniformly coated in matt cream stone-paint. This may seem brutal to those who can remember the purple-painted cloak from over 20 years ago, even if cream seems more appropriate to Quaker ideals.

The statue seems to be firmly gazing towards Norwich Cathedral in the east but if it were to turn about 45 degrees to the right she would see her house somewhere at the junction of Opie Street with Castle Meadow. The memorial plaque on the front of the house says that she 'lived in this or an adjacent house'

As a Quaker, Amelia began to campaign against the slave trade and, together with Anna Gurney, set up the Norwich branch of a national network of female anti-slavery societies. A few years after the Slavery Abolition Act was passed (1833) Amelia attended the World Anti-Slavery Convention in London (1840). In Benjamin Haydon's picture of the event Amelia Opie sits amongst other women, standing out in her high, black Quaker bonnet.

Sculpture of Mrs Opie by Z Leon in Opie Street

The Anti-Slavery Convention (1840) by Benjamin Haydon. Wikimedia Commons.

The south-east corner of Opie Street (circled) and Castle Meadow

Amelia Opie died aged 84 and is buried beside her father in the Quaker Burial Ground in Gildencroft, off St Augustine's Street. The Gurneys congregate in the far corner.

Harriet Martineau by Richard Evans 1834. Public Domain

Harriet Martineau (1802-1876) was born into a family of Norwich Unitarians. Unitarians were Dissenters who rejected the concept of god as a trinity in favour of a less dogmatic religion guided by individual conscience.

Of French Huguenot descent, the family is commemorated by Martineau Lane near County Hall. This is not named for Harriet's but for her uncle, Dr Philip Meadows Martineau, who owned nearby Bracondale Hall and Carrow Abbey. The family name is also displayed on the Martineau Memorial Hall and Sunday School in Colegate but refers to Harriet's younger brother James (1805-1900) who established the school next to the Unitarian Octagon Chapel where their father was deacon. Despite being surrounded in her formative years by religion, albeit a dissenting one, Harriet eventually became a secularist when she was exposed to Charles Darwin's ideas.

The Martineau Memorial Hall in Colegate

Memorial plaque to Elizabeth Fry and Harriet Martineau, born in the same building on Magdalen Street.

Norwich has an Elizabeth Fry Road and an Opie Street but we must look to Thomas Paine's home town of Thetford to find Harriet Martineau Close. Harriet's own name can just be glimpsed though the bars of the gated alleyway to Gurney House in Magdalen Street where she and Elizabeth Fry had been born.

At home, Harriet and her three sisters were educated to the same level as their four brothers except the young men then went out into the world while the young women were expected to stay at home – an injustice that Harriet addressed in an article *'On Female Education'* in the *Unitarian Monthly Repository*. She had been a sensitive and poorly child; deaf from age twelve she used an ear trumpet throughout her life. After her father died when Harriet was in her twenties she was forced to earn a living, which she eventually achieved through her writing. In 1832 she moved to London where she was lionised by the city's intellectual circles, meeting economist Malthus, geologist Lyell, philosopher John Stuart Mill, mathematician Charles Babbage, Charles Darwin's brother Erasmus, and novelists Elizabeth Barrett Browning and George Eliot. In the capital she published an enormously popular commentary to Adam Smith's ideas in *Illustrations of Political Economy*, which ran to 25 volumes and outsold several of Dickens' novels. This was followed by *Poor Laws and Paupers Illustrated and Illustrations of Taxation*.

Surprisingly for someone who had been a sickly child, Harriet Martineau spent two years travelling in the 1830s. Instead of enjoying the civilised amenities of Europe she decided to rough it by observing the new democracy of the United States, much as Amelia Opie had travelled to Paris in 1802 to see Republicanism in action. Harriet's experiences in the new world were published in Society in America (1837) in which she was outspoken in her call for racial equality and – concerned about the lack of education for American women – female rights.

Harriet Martineau was a radical whose relentless activism led Charles Dickens to say of her that she was,'grimly bent upon the enlightenment of mankind'. This burning concern for social reform ranged widely over what have become separate disciplines. Nowadays she is recognised as the first female sociologist and a pioneer of that field of study. She was also one of the first women journalists, having earned her living by her pen since her twenties and joining the staff of *The Daily News* in 1852. In later life, after an argument with her brother, Harriet moved to Ambleside in the Lake District. She died in 1876 and was buried in the Martineau family grave in Birmingham

Madness was an all-enveloping term whose varieties can affect us all and for which we now have much kinder words. A jarring name, much used up to the eighteenth century, it was replaced by 'insanity' in the nineteenth century and 'mental illness' in the twentieth. I began this blog post during Mental Health Awareness Week in May 2021 when my thoughts turned to a family member who had Alzheimer's disease. I was also reminded of some of the subjects I'd written about in this blog and wondered how they would have been cared for in less enlightened times.

John Joseph Cotman. Landscape with Sun Set, Haystacks and Owl.
Courtesy of Mandell's Gallery, Norwich

The leading figure in the Norwich School of Painters, John Sell Cotman (1728-1842) occupies prime position in the city's pantheon yet, it is thought, he never achieved full recognition at the national level because of his intermittently manic personality. Now recognised as bipolar disorder, these extremes of elation and depression also affected Cotman's sons. Miles Edmund, who often finished his father's paintings, was depressive; Alfred's violent behaviour led to his committal in an asylum; and John Joseph was known around the city, rather cruelly, as Crazy Cotman. His brilliantly colourful and energetic paintings are the antithesis of the calmness portrayed in the wherry school of painting. A local GP described his paintings as shocking: 'like the sight of a brightly dressed demi-mondaine at a gathering of Quakers … an Expressionist before his time'.

A little more is known about the troubled life of Thomas Jeckyll, born eight years after Alfred Cotman and subject of four blog posts. Wymondham-born Jeckyll became an important figure in the Aesthetic Movement based on the fashion for Japanese art, spearheaded by the painter Whistler. Earlier in his career, Jeckyll had worked for his patron, Sir John Boileau of Ketteringham Hall, during which time he was seen as unreliable. A later absence was to precipitate the infamous affair of the Peacock Room. Due to illness, Jeckyll had to absent himself from a project to design a room in the London house of wealthy collector Frederick Leyland, where he could display his oriental china. Whistler, who had been working elsewhere in the house, completed Jeckyll's work but he went far beyond any ideas discussed with Leyland. The Peacock Room, in blue and gold, is a masterpiece achieved by painting over the surfaces of Jeckyll's room and, in so doing, effectively airbrushing Jeckyll's contribution from history. Only a pair of sunflower fire irons remain as a reminder of the Norfolk artist.

Thomas Jeckyll returned from London to the family home in Unthank Road, Norwich. He had been experiencing pressure of work in the early 1870s and in 1873 underwent some kind of crisis. In November 1876, having suffered his first manic episode, he was admitted to Heigham Hall.

In searching for Heigham Hall in Mason's Directory of 1852 I came across 'Asylum-lane' in the parish of Heigham. We know this now as Park Lane, off Unthank Road, but then you would have had to travel on through open countryside before arriving at the extensive wooded grounds of Heigham Hall, Private Lunatic Asylum. Situated about half a mile out of the city at the junction with Dereham Road, the Hall – formerly the

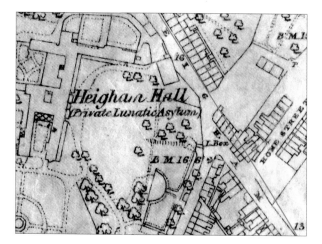
Heigham Hall (Private Lunatic Asylum), junction of Old Palace Rd and Heigham Rd (red line). Ordnance Survey 1884. Courtesy of Norfolk Libraries and Information Services.

Marrowbone House/Hall. Bryant's Map 1826. Courtesy of Norfolk Record Office.

been like a gentleman's mansion, inside and out, and it was here that Jeckyll was incarcerated.

Although Thomas Jeckyll's condition seems not to have improved, he was discharged from Marrowbone Hall the following year to his father's home in Norwich. However, George Jeckell (whose spelling of his surname betrays the son's fancified 'y'), was himself exhibiting signs of mania and died in May 1878. A few months prior to this Thomas had been incarcerated in the city's Bethel Hospital as a fee-paying patient and he was to stay here until his death in 1881. As we saw for the Cotmans, inheritance plays a strong part in bipolar disorder.

In 1852, the Reverend Edmund Holmes was found in bed with the 12-year-old daughter of Mrs Bunn, his housekeeper, who called the constable. Holmes was taken to a magistrate who referred him for committal to Heigham Hall. Just a few months later Holmes was discharged and immediately became a boarder with a post as the asylum's chaplain. The public were incensed that the owners appeared to have offered a dubious diagnosis of insanity so that a man from 'a high county family' could evade the law. A surprisingly partisan article in a medical journal of 1855 tried to boost Heigham Hall's reputation, stating that others had agreed Holmes was a lunatic and that the housekeeper's husband had often held the minister on the floor as a protection from violence.

old Grange – was partly renovated by John Lowden around 1810 'in modern style'. Lowden made his money as a contractor to the army in the Napoleonic Wars and Bryant's map of 1826 gives a sly dig to this by labelling the property, Marrowbone House.

In 1836, Drs John Ferra Watson and William Peter Nichols opened the hall as a private mental home for 'patients belonging to the upper and middle classes'. Set in 12 acres of ornamental grounds it was said to have

Heigham Hall. Courtesy of Norfolk Record Office

The affair became a national cause célèbre when another doctor claimed that Dr Watson of Heigham Hall had offered him a bribe to sign Holmes' lunacy certificate, saying it would be worth 'hundreds a year in his pocket'. Following questions in Parliament, the Lunacy Act was amended so that no-one's status as a patient could be switched to boarder without full investigation by the Commissioners in Lunacy. But the question remained: was this the ploy of a wealthy man to evade justice or was Holmes insane?

Heigham Retreat. Etching by Henry Ninham (d. 1874).
Courtesy of Norfolk Record Office.

From 1904 until his death in 1949, Heigham Hall was owned by Dr John Gordon Gordon-Munn who, in 1914/15 was Lord Mayor of Norwich. As a trainee doctor he had written a short thesis on, 'Some Observations Upon the Uterus and its Appendages in the Insane.' That is, he examined the macro- and microscopic appearance of the sexual organs of insane women. In his brief introduction, he cites various sources to support his assertion that, 'It has long been held that a decided relation does exist between pathological conditions of the sexual apparatus in women and insanity.' This offers a disturbing insight into the prevailing (male) view of 'women's problems' that persisted into the twentieth century. Women were thought to be liable to a periodic lunacy according to the lunar cycle – the waxing and waning of the moon. The Latin for moon, 'lunaris', gives rise to 'loony' while the Latin for womb, 'hystericus,' is evidently the base for 'hysterical'. Indeed, there were claims that female hysteria could be cured by hysterectomy. In 1866 a physician wrote that clitoridectomy could cure certain kinds of insanity. Such barbaric treatment appears to be the product of sympathetic magic, not science.

Heigham Hall had set itself up as competition with an establishment near Park Lane known as Heigham Retreat – the word 'retreat' signifying its use as a private asylum. It was approached from Park Lane along an avenue of trees that gave name to present-day Avenue Road. In 1859, the proprietors of Heigham Hall bought out their competitors at Heigham Retreat and promptly closed it. Now, Avenue Junior School occupies the

site. Heigham Hall itself lasted until 1960 when it was demolished to make way for Dolphin Grove social housing.

Five miles west of the city, Costessey Hall was home to the Jerninghams on whose land George Gunton established the brickworks whose carved and moulded fancy bricks helped define the face of Victorian Norwich. Before they spread through Victorian Norwich and beyond, Gunton's Cossey Reds were used first to build the phantasmagorical Hall. Commissioned by Lord Stafford and designed by JC Buckler it was one of the most convincing examples of the Gothic Revival style. The building was raised over a decade (1826-1836) but was never completed and was still being demolished a century later.

Costessey Hall. Credit: costesseypark.com

The 10th Baron Stafford, Sir Augustus Frederick Fitzherbert Stafford Jerningham was probably the grandson of Mrs Fitzherbert and the Prince Regent (the future George IV). Jerningham was certified insane by the Lunacy Commission. Whether or not his mental illness was inherited from the Hanovers is unclear but some hereditary component seemed to run in the family for Jerningham's younger brother, Sir Fitzosbert Edward Stafford Jerningham, was considered to be eccentric. He threw out watches that failed to keep time and rarely ventured outside, reasoning that his brother had left the park and never returned.

Ordinary individuals had no wealth to insulate them from physical or mental illness. The earliest public asylum in the country was Bethlehem Hospital, which moved from just outside London's city walls to Moorfields in 1676. Although the Bethel Hospital in Norwich came later (1713) it had the distinction of being the country's first purpose-built asylum. This is where Thomas Jeckyll spent his last years.

Bethel Hospital, Bethel Street side

The austere external facade on Bethel Street is part of Edward Boardman's remodelling in the Queen Anne style (1899). The Bethel Street side, with small. high-set windows conveyed a sense of imprisonment, while inside the walls there were gardens and a ladies' croquet lawn.

The original building was founded by Mary Chapman, daughter of John Mann, a wealthy worsted merchant who had been the city's mayor and the county's high sheriff. This was on the site of the Committee House that stored the county's arms during the Civil War. In 1648, during a popular Royalist uprising against troopers of the New Model Army, citizens broke into the building and somehow ignited 98 barrels of gunpowder. The explosion, or 'Great Blow', killed around 100 people and blew out the glass in the nearby churches of St Stephens and St Peter Mancroft. The churchwarden's accounts for St Peter Mancroft record that in 1652 the 'glasyer' William Rutter was paid 13 pounds, four shillings and sixpence 'for the glaseing of the sayd East windowe and other glasing work in the church'. Rutter's east window would have been a collection of fifteenth century glass, painted in several Norwich workshops, and rescued from around the church.

Mary Chapman's husband, John, was rector of the parish church of Thorpe to the east of the city. Both had mental illness in their families and John left money to found a charity for those deprived of their reason. Mary was to use her remaining 24 years to build The Bethel on the site of the old Committee Rooms and establish a hospital for the insane. The patients' relatives were expected to pay what they could and during Mary Chapman's lifetime she herself paid for the maintenance of several inmates. Her will arranged for a trust to provide 'not for natural born idiots or fools, but for the convenient reception and habitation of lunatics'. This provides a rough distinction between conditions apparent at birth and those that appeared later in life, although it is now known that the latter may have a genetic basis.

'The Madhouse'. Plate VIII of The Rake's progress by Wm Hogarth. Public domain.

In 1735, William Hogarth published his engravings of The Rake's Progress in which Tom Rakewell ends up violent and deranged in The Madhouse (Plate VIII). Hogarth's print has its own taxonomy of madness and is instructive for illustrating attitudes to, and classification of, mental disturbance in the mid-eighteenth century. Having led a dissolute life, Tom Rakewell (front left), sits on the floor with a self-inflicted wound in his side and is being chained for his own protection. The man on the stairs (right), in love with a famous courtesan, is besotted, lovelorn, moonstruck. The tailor (centre mid-ground) measures an imaginary client with his tape. Two cells are occupied by delusional patients. The terms used to describe these different species of mental illness might not stand up to modern scrutiny but we should remember that science was yet to get into its stride. As a benchmark for where this stands in the history of science, the man at the back, part-hidden by the door, is trying to find a method for what seemed to be the intractable problem of determining longitude and, in case we didn't grasp this, Hogarth has written the word on the wall. The man kneeling with a makeshift telescope to his eye is probably trying to solve the longitude problem by observing the stars. Two years after Hogarth published his print, the Longitude Commissioners awarded John Harrison a prize for producing a chronometer accurate enough to measure the difference in local time – and hence longitude – between a ship at sea and Greenwich Mean Time.

The two fashionably-dressed young women have come to visit, one of them using her fan to block sight of a crowned man with a sceptre in one hand and said to be urinating with the aid of the other. While the visiting elite could claim to be motivated by higher ideals, and were expected to make a charitable contribution towards the upkeep of the insane, crowds of the lower sort would come to 'Bedlam' in search of amusement. Madness was a diversion.

'Madness' and 'lunacy' – terms offensive to modern ears – were everyday coin in the eighteenth century; in the nineteenth century they were largely replaced by 'insanity' and in the twentieth century by 'mental illness'. Historian Steven Cherry also makes the distinction between madness as a legal term and mental illness as a medical concept. In a more religious age, madness could be perceived to be the consequences of 'sinfulness and the loss of divine protection'. Another explanation, set out by the Ancient Greeks, suggested that temperament was regulated by an imbalance of the four bodily humours: blood, phlegm, yellow bile and black bile. An excess of black bile was thought to cause melancholia whereas a choleric and manic nature was attributed to an excess of yellow bile. The humoral theory held for two millennia but had little or no practical use in treating: hysteria, post-natal depression, schizophrenia, epilepsy, the effects of syphilis on the brain, monomania (e.g., conversing with supernatural beings), congenital idiocy, delirium tremens caused by alcohol etc etc. The madness of King George the Third had been attributed to the blood disorder, porphyria, which may have been treated with arsenic, but a twenty-first century analysis of his handwriting suggests that the monarch could have been exhibiting acute mania.

In the late eighteenth century two figures carved by Caius Gabriel Cibber decorated the pediment over the gates of London's Bethlem Hospital. These depicted the two poles of manic depression: 'melancholy madness' and 'raving madness' and were evidently the model for Hogarth's final image of Tom Rakewell.

On Samuel King's map of 1766, the Norwich asylum was labelled a dignified, biblical Bethel although the road outside was named Bedlam Street, with its connotation of chaos.

From a young age, Amelia Opie visited the Bethel Hospital. She would throw a halfpenny over the wall for an inmate, Goodings, to buy snuff. She also spent most of her weekly allowance buying him pinks and other flowers after he had admired a nosegay she was wearing. Despite being petrified by his clanking chains she could still write, 'Some of my happiest moments were those when I visited the gates of bedlam.' As a romantic 16-year-old, Amelia went inside the Bethel with two male friends at a time when she 'considered madness not as occasioned by some physical derangement, but as the result, in most cases, of moral causes.' But young Amelia

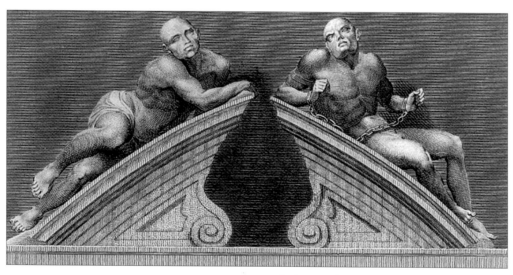

On the gates of Bethlem Hospital, London 1784. Public domain

(a) Sir Benjamin Wrench by D Heins(?) 1747. Wellcome Collection; Public domain.
(b) Sir Benjamin Wrench's Court by Henry Ninham, early C19; Wikimedia Commons.

saw no lovelorn patients rolling their eyes and 'went away disappointed from having false ideas of the nature of the affliction which we had gone to contemplate.'

It may be surprising to read from Amelia Opie's account that inmates of the Bethel, who were free to roam the grounds, might still be chained. Inmates were owed a sense of duty and humanity and 'in obstinate resistances to be governed no blows or correction with any weapon.' But records show that humane management still involved handcuffs, padlocks, a heavy chair with straps, and straight-waistcoats. Chains were intended to prevent escape and to minimise harm but were insufficient to stop a patient from killing the Master, James Bullard, with a scythe.

Surgeon doctors attended patients in the Bethel, some from the Norfolk and Norwich Hospital founded in 1771 just outside the St Stephen's Gate on St Stephens Road. The first physician to be appointed was Sir Benjamin

Wrench who promised Mary Chapman that he would continue in his medical role at the Bethel for as long as he was able. He retired in 1747 aged 82. The physician's house in Sir Benjamin Wrench's Court was where the Norwich Society of Artists held their first exhibition. The building was demolished in 1826 to make way for the new Corn Exchange on the corner of Exchange and Little Bedford Streets, where the north end of Jarrold Department Store now stands. As for the Bethel itself, it became an annexe of the City Asylum at Hellesdon when the NHS was established in 1948. The hospital closed in 1995 after 282 years service and has been converted to private apartments.

At the beginning of the nineteenth century, Norwich had approximately 50 private asylums and a handful of private subscription asylums. The 'lunatic poor' went to the poor house or workhouse even though there was no special provision for them. However, from 1828, they were to be housed on a site once occupied by a lazar

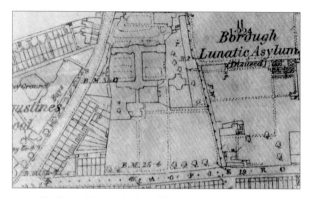

The Borough Lunatic Asylum off Magpie Rd (red line). OS map 1886; Norfolk Libraries and Information Services.

(leper) hospital established by a Bishop of Norwich; this was just outside the city wall at St Augustine's Gates in a new building that had a ward for the sick. The new asylum, adjacent to the pre-existing workhouse infirmary, was known for the first two years of its existence as the Norwich Pauper Asylum. Renamed the Norwich City Asylum, the institution was to remain here until 1880 when the city's accommodation for

the mentally ill was transferred to new premises at Hellesdon. Six years after this the Ordnance Survey showed that the old site in St Augustine's was still disused. The adjacent workhouse infirmary, however, had already left the site in 1859 for Bowthorpe Road, forming the nucleus of what would become the West Norwich Hospital with a ward for lunatics

Public mental health provision was therefore moving out beyond the immediate confines of a congested medieval city. Although not in Norwich itself, the Norfolk Lunatic Asylum at Thorpe St Andrews, had already been opened two and half miles east of the city centre in 1814. This was one of the newly decreed County Asylums and only the third of its kind in the country. Established as a result of an Act of 1808, it was paid for by the county rates, specifically for pauper and criminal lunatics. We see it in an engraving by John Berney Ladbrooke, son of co-founder of the Norwich Society of Artists, Robert Ladbrooke.

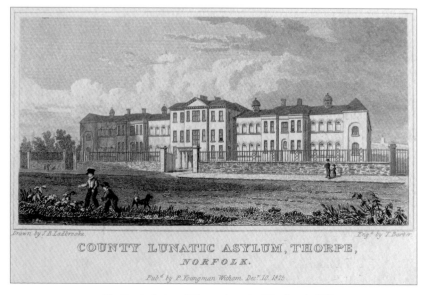

The County Asylum at Thorpe, drawn by JB Ladbrooke 1825. Courtesy of David Clarke.

At one time Britain's sea defences faced south, towards France and Spain, but when Napoleon occupied Holland our sights turned eastwards to possible invasion from the North Sea and the Baltic. To counter this, a naval base was established at Great Yarmouth in 1796 and rapid communication with the Admiralty in London required something more than flags and burning barrels of tar.

In the seventeenth century, Robert Hooke suggested that the recently invented telescope could be used to read secret messages. I can't show you a portrait of Doctor Hooke for he fell out with Sir Isaac Newton – President of the recently-formed Royal Society – about his contribution to the Theory of Gravity and some have argued that a vengeful Newton ensured that no image of Hooke remained.

Hooke was in the first wave of natural philosophers to use an effective compound microscope based on the magnifying power of two or more lenses. He is known to modern microscopists for coining the term 'cell' for the magnified holes he saw in sections of cork for these reminded him of monks' cells in a monastery. But Robert Hooke is probably more generally known for having used his microscope to draw a flea, signalling the fact that these experiments in optics took place in the year of the Great Plague.

The first successful practical use of the telescope to convey messages over long distances was developed by the Frenchman Claude Chappe, who coined the term 'semaphore' (Greek: sēma = sign; phoros = carrying). At the beginning of the nineteenth century the French could communicate rapidly between Paris, Lille and Brussels

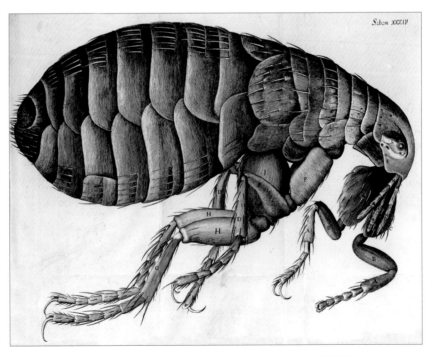

Flea, from Robert Hooke's Micrographia 1665. Wikimedia Commons.

using Chappe's semaphore system that eventually covered the whole of France and even extended to Amsterdam and Venice. Each station consisted of a tower from which protruded a mast holding movable arms that spelled out a code to be read by telescope; by the next station, some 10-20 miles away.

In 1795 the Bishop of St David's in Wales, Lord George Murray, offered a different model to the British Admiralty, for which he was awarded £2000. This consisted of a six-metre-high shutter frame with three pairs of metre-square panels. Each swivelling panel could be pulled by ropes and flipped between edge-on (in which case that panel appeared empty and light) or face-on (when the blocked panel appeared dark), producing sixty four combinations. Unlike the Chappe system, in which each setting corresponded to a coded message, Murray combinations corresponded to single letters and could spell out words. For instance, six 'open' panels signified the latter A and six 'closed' panels signified 'C'.

These shutter stations might consist of a living room, a room for operations, a small garden and coal shed. Four to six naval men ran the station in twos or threes

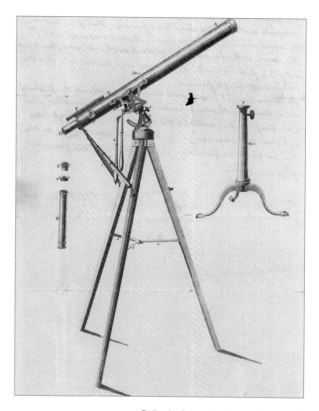

Dolland achromatic telescope. Public domain

with one manning the shutters while the other(s) looked through high-power telescopes. Because the rainbow colours that make up white light have different wavelengths it is difficult to focus them to the same point through a lens, producing a blurred images with a colour fringe. But in 1758 John Dollond (d.1761) – son of a Huguenot silk weaver in Spitalfields, London – patented a compound lens that improved the telescope. He cemented a concave lens of flint glass to a convex lens of crown glass, which largely overcame this chromatic aberration. The Admiralty shutter telegraph used Dollond telescopes, possibly their top-of-the-range 'Twelve Guinea' instrument. (Dollond's optical business became Dollond and Aitchison in 1927 and merged with Boots Opticians in 2009).

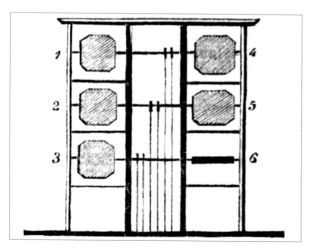

The Murray shutter telegraph 1795. Wikimedia Commons.

The first experimental station, built in Portsmouth in 1795, was the start of the line to Deal consisting of 15 relay stations; it took another 10 years to extend to Plymouth. Relay stations were 7-10 miles apart but the 1808 line to Great Yarmouth involved intervals up to 11.7 miles and required three right-angle bends, including one at Norwich. Anticipating problems of mist and fog over low-lying ground the contractor, George Roebuck, avoided a line through Essex. Instead, the line turned north-west out of London to the Chilterns, before finally heading north-east into East Anglia. A message from the Admiralty to Yarmouth took 17 minutes.

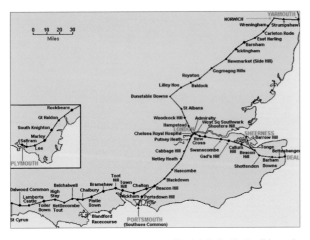

The Admiralty Shutter Telegraph.
©Norfolk Industrial Archaeology Society. With permission.

The first station inside Norfolk was in East Harling but before investigating the site I visited the church and its many treasures of the Late Middle Ages. The east window contains the best rural collection of fifteenth century painted glass from John Wighton's Norwich workshop, which also made the glass for St Peter Mancroft, Norwich. By 1460 the workshop was run by John Mundeford, from a family of Dutch emigrés, whose father William had also led the Wighton workshop. Hidden away in the tracery of the east window is a fuzzy squirrel whose siblings can be seen on the shield of the Lovell family tomb-chest in the nave. The animal

provides a clue to the identity of the woman who sat for Holbein's enigmatic 'Portrait of a Lady with a Starling and a Squirrel'. (See opposite.)

David King, historian of stained glass, who comes from a family of Norwich glass restorers, recognised the squirrel as an emblem of the Lovell family. He suggested that the starling was a pun on East Harling, which could be spelled Estharlyng in the sixteenth century. The sitter may therefore be Anne, wife of Sir Francis Lovell (d. 1551) who was Esquire to the Body of Henry VIII – a man well-placed to have commissioned Holbein on his first visit to England.

When I did get to the former site of the shutter telegraph station (1808-14) it was up a gentle East Anglian slope about a mile out of town. The first edition OS map reminds us that a Telegraph House stood nearby. Telegraph Farm offers a clue to the next location at Carleton Rode but the station itself seems to have been at Telegraph Pit to the south-east of the farm itself.

Driving across a land unrelieved by anything approaching a proper hill forces one to think how shutters on top of a hut could ever be seen ten miles away. In an article published in the Journal of the Norfolk Industrial Archaeology Society (2001), Bernard Ambrose addressed this by plotting the cross-sections between stations using the contours on OS maps. The

All Saints Wreningham

Portrait of a Lady with a Starling and a Squirrel, by Hans Holbein the Younger ca. 1526. National Gallery. Wikimedia Commons

fact that a line of sight was possible only if modern-day shrubs and hedges were removed gives a sense of how difficult it is to see distant terrain across these flatlands and explains the preoccupation of East Anglian painters with big skies.

The next station was thought to have been at Wreningham, 'on high ground near the church', but Ambrose found difficulties with this attribution. Instead of a shutter station near Wreningham All Saints, he proposed that a lost church – St Mary's, formerly marked on OS maps – was the actual site. But according to Faden's map of 1797 a large ancient wood to the west of Ashwellthorpe would have blocked the line of sight. Inspection of Bryant's map, however, shows that by

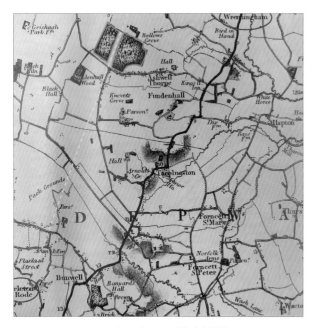

Bryant's map of Norfolk 1826. Norfolk Record Office.

decades ago by Dutch elm disease. I recall the rookery in the giant elms louring over my daughter's kindergarten. Once, when I drove in late, spraying gravel over the carpark, the commotion catapulted birds out of their nests. 'Look,' my daughter said, 'pepper in the sky'. Elms have gone and now the ash of Ashwellthorpe are heading that way.

From Wreningham, the telegraph line continues north-east to Norwich. In 1803 a commercial telegraph station had been erected on top of Norwich Castle for signalling to Yarmouth but this earlier project was abandoned because smoke from the city affected visibility. In Norwich Castle Museum there is an echo of Ashwellthorpe in the form of a triptych by the Master of the Magdalen Legend (ca 1483-ca 1530). The Ashwellthorpe Triptych, also known as the Seven Sorrows of Mary, was commissioned by Christopher Knyvet of Ashwellthorpe when Henry VIII sent him to The Netherlands.

1826 a drive had been cut through Ashwellthorpe Wood (outlined in green), perhaps to provide a line of sight for the shutter telegraph.

Ashwellthorpe Wood, mentioned in the Domesday Book, has endured since the Anglo-Saxon period but in 2012 the silent invasion of ash dieback disease from the continent initiated sudden changes. A scientist from the John Innes Centre in Norwich, Anne Edwards, was a volunteer at the wood and used molecular techniques to confirm, for the first time, the presence of ash dieback disease in the UK. The wood contains 40% ash trees so, even if some are resistant, the balance of native broadleaved trees will be transformed, as it was some

The actual site of the Admiralty Telegraph in Norwich was near the present-day water tower at the top of Telegraph Lane in Thorpe St Andrews, about 2 km east of the city centre and 15 km north-east of Wreningham [Fig 13.8]. The 1886 OS map shows two features In the vicinity of the water tower with the name 'telegraph': Telegraph Cottages and Telegraph Plantation. In a visit to the Norfolk Record Office I found a plan of Telegraph Cottage, Thorpe, owned in 1858 by the Harvey family of Crown Point. This is almost certainly the shutter station and provides a rare plan of the layout. The building of brick and weatherboard was comprised of three storeys (basement, ground floor and chamber) and was only 20 feet wide and 13 feet deep. Windows are placed along the east-west axis.

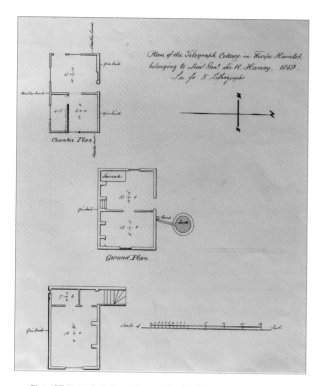

Plan of Telegraph Cottage, Thorpe Hamlet, Norwich. Norfolk Record Office.

Telegraph Hill ca. 2miles north of Honingham village

At 220 feet the ridge overlooking Norwich from the east is high for Norfolk and was the vantage point from which Robert Kett's rebels fired upon the city in 1549. You would imagine, therefore, that this ridge would be ideal for signalling but Ambrose suggested that the line of sight between Wreningham and the Thorpe shutter station might have been sensitive to smoke from the city or to mists over low-lying ground to the south. To get around this problem he proposed, counterintuitively, that a reserve shutter station was sited to the west of the city. This explains the presence of Telegraph Hill near Honingham – to the west – but signals from that station would still have to penetrate the atmospheric pollution over Norwich city in order to be read by the Norwich station at Thorpe. So perhaps mists over the low-lying riverland south of Norwich were really the problem. Whichever way they arrived at Norwich, signals from the south had to be redirected eastwards to Yarmouth and to achieve this the shutters were either larger than usual (so that they could be seen at an angle) or the station had two shutter frames facing different directions.

The last shutter station before Yarmouth was at Strumpshaw where there is a tump – a proper little hill just south of the church. Previously a site for sand and gravel extraction it is now a recycling centre. Driving down the west side of this wooded slope I found a waypost pointing westward to a distant Norwich. With the aid of a struggling zoom lens I could just make out Telegraph Hill in Thorpe and St Peter Mancroft in the city centre.

In 1798, King George III sent a message to both Houses of Parliament stating that preparations were being made by the French for the invasion of this kingdom. This was seven years before the Battle of Trafalgar and 17 years before Waterloo and it is hard for us now to appreciate the widespread fear of an invasion by the French revolutionary Army, especially on the east coast. In response, the Yarmouth Corporation voted £500 towards the town's preparations and granted the Admiralty a piece of ground on the South Denes 'for the convenience of naval officers and men to attend the signals.'

Great Yarmouth has one of the best-preserved medieval town-walls, dating back to 1261 when Henry II granted the right to enclose the settlement. Eleven defensive towers remain, including the South-East Tower. However, the South Gate, where the shutter station was based, has not survived. Palmer's History records, 'A small wooden hut was erected, which after the war was occupied by the inspecting commander of the coast guard'. This hut would appear to be illustrated below. A private residence, Telegraph House, was later built on the enlarged site and demolished in the 1950s.

Lantern slide 'South Gate with Telegraph' ca.1807. Norfolk Record Office

In 1814 the shutter stations were sold after Napoleon was defeated and banished to Elba. When Napoleon escaped, the Portsmouth and Deal shutter lines were replaced with a semaphore system but not the Yarmouth - London branch, in recognition of the diminished threat to Norfolk shores after the defeat of the French navy at Trafalgar. In 1817-19, the 44-metre high Nelson

(or Britannia) Monument was raised not far from the Yarmouth shutter station. Nelson's column in Trafalgar Square is topped by the man himself while, in Yarmouth, Britannia looks inland towards Nelson's birthplace at Burnham Thorpe in North Norfolk.

The Britannia Monument, Great Yarmouth (1817-19).

The ancient freedoms granted Norwich by the Crown created a sense of independence that often tripped into outright opposition against church and state. Dissent may have been woven into the fabric of this city but after the Reformation the extent of your opposition to the Anglican Church would have decided whether or not you could be buried in your local churchyard.

Following the Reformation, Nonconformist factions like the Baptists, Methodists, Presbyterians and Quakers were discriminated against by the Established Church for, despite having to pay church rates, Dissenters were still refused burial in their local churchyard. An Act of 1836 allowed Nonconformists to conduct their own funerals but it wasn't until 1880 that they had the right to be buried in a parish church, using their own rites instead of a Church of England service.

According to the 2011 census, Norwich was the country's most godless city. The pattern was already set by the time of the 1851 census when the majority of Norwich citizens attended neither church nor chapel. As long ago as the early eighteenth century – when there may have been good reasons for not declaring your religious convictions – 20% of the Norwich population were classed as Dissenters, and that figure would rise. Nonconformist chapels therefore tended to be built with their own burial grounds. The Octagon Chapel in Colegate, designed by Thomas Ivory in 1756 to replace a Presbyterian meeting house of 1686, was the first of its kind in the country but its abandonment of the cross-shaped plan in favour of the octagon led it to be called 'The Devil's Cucumber Frame'. Visitors to the small garden at the Octagon will walk on a path composed of fragments of headstones, betraying the presence of a former burial ground. But there were no burials after 1821, the significance of which comes later.

In Norwich, The Society of Friends (The Quakers) originally met in private houses or in the open air but

Octagon Chapel garden

in 1676 they bought a modest quarter of an acre in Goat Lane where they were to build a meeting house. By 1700 their congregation had grown to around 500 so the Friends built a second meeting house in Gildencroft, in Norwich-Over-the-Water, next to an acre of land already used for their burial ground.

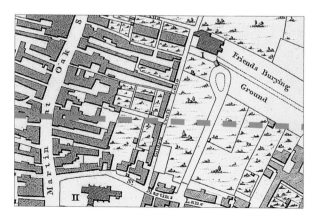

Millard & Manning's plan of Norwich 1830. Dotted line = ring road.
Norfolk Record Office.

Access to the burial ground via narrow Gildencroft Lane (now Quakers Lane) was difficult for pall bearers and so the Quakers rented land between the burial ground and St Martins (or Whores) Lane off Oak Street to allow horse-drawn wagons to bear the coffin. This strip of land with a wagon-turning circle at the north end can be seen on a city plan of 1830; modern maps will show the lane bisected by the inner link road of the 1970s (dotted line on map). The meeting house was bombed in 1942 and replaced by a children's centre though a ghost of the turning circle remains in the form of the crescent-shaped wall adjoining the burial ground.

Congregation used a larger eighteenth century cemetery at the top of Horn's Lane, off Ber Street. This was high on the hill above the synagogue on Synagogue Street, which had been the only road in the country to bear this name. It was bombed in World War Two. George Plunkett photographed the Jewish Gildencroft cemetery in 1937, five years before the Luftwaffe bombed the Quaker Meeting House, which can be seen in the background. As you drive eastwards on the dual carriageway at St Crispin's Road, look left for a small stone tablet that commemorates the former Jewish cemetery behind the wall.

Oak St/Talbot Square Hebrew cemetery ©georgeplunkett.co.uk

A vestige of the turning circle.

Near Quakers Lane in Gildencroft, between the inner ring road and Talbot Square, is the site of a small Jewish cemetery established in 1813 but closed when the corporation opened its nondenominational cemetery at Earlham in 1856. Before this, the county's Hebrew

To side-step the obstacles surrounding dissenting burials the Unitarian minister, Thomas Drummond, established The Rosary Cemetery at Thorpe in in 1819. He seems to have been motivated by his time in Ipswich when a curate refused a funeral service in the parish church for a young child who Drummond himself had baptised. The Rosary was the first cemetery in the country where anyone could be buried irrespective of religion and without having to be supervised by an Anglican minister. The first occupant was Drummond's wife, Ann, disinterred from the Octagon Chapel whose own burial ground soon became disused.

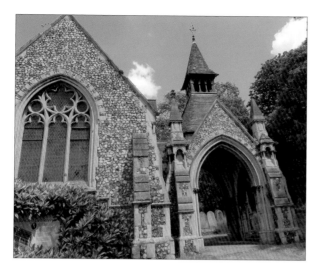

The Rosary chapel and carriage porch

The City Surveyor, JS Benest, designed The Rosary lodge in 1860 but this was redesigned in 1879 by Edward Boardman; he also designed the mortuary chapel and its carriage porch in the Victorian Gothic style. Boardman (1834-1910), who probably did more to modernise the medieval city than any other architect, was himself buried at The Rosary.

Boardman's son and partner, Edward Thomas Boardman, married Florence, daughter of Jeremiah James Colman (1830-1898), managing director of the family mustard business. In 1898, Jeremiah James' funeral cortège included his firm's horse-drawn wagons followed by 1200 workers from the Carrow Works. Although Protestant he made a point of holding services for his workers on non-denominational lines and in the same spirit the family's memorial stones are simply worded – factual and secular. Several members of the Colman family are buried in the family plot. Its Celtic Cross – and there are several at The Rosary – might imply a distancing from traditional Anglican symbolism but inscriptions on the obelisk rectify any such impression with reminders of the Christian afterlife (e.g., 'I know that my redeemer liveth').

The Colman family plot at The Rosary

Jeremiah Cozens' cast-iron sarcophagus

The Jarrold monument

One of the memorial stones unites Jeremiah James and Caroline Colman with their son Alan Cozens-Hardy Colman. Alan died in Egypt and, in his memory, his sisters Ethel and Helen built the pleasure wherry Hathor – the name borrowed from the Nile boat on which he had been convalescing from tuberculosis. Hathor's interior contains decoration in the Ancient Egyptian style, designed by Boardman. When Hathor was launched on the Norfolk Broads in 1905, Edward Thomas and Florence Boardman's three and a half-year-old daughter Joan released doves.

The Colmans were caring and paternalistic employers, providing workers with health insurance, the first industrial nurse, and housing and schooling for the children. Their many good works, however, go unsung at The Rosary and there is a reticence in their

celebration of death. You would never guess from the plain inscription (name, parents, where born, where died) on a simple stone that their second daughter Ethel Mary (1863-1948), who campaigned for female suffrage, became the first lady Lord Mayor (1923) in Norwich and, indeed, Great Britain.

Jeremiah Cozens (d. 1849), whose niece married JJ Colman, has the only cast-iron sarcophagus at The Rosary.

One of the first memorials you encounter after entering the carriage porch is dedicated to the Jarrold family of Dutch or Huguenot origin. John Jarrold II started out as a printer and bookseller in Woodbridge, Suffolk. After seeing Dissenters attending services in Wickham Market being stoned by unruly mobs, John Jarrold was drawn into defending the right to public worship. In 1823, he

Emanuel Cooper's mausoleum

Hines family members

moved to Norwich, opening Jarrold & Son in London Street where it remains, still selling books 200 years later.

The only mausoleum at The Rosary belongs to Emanuel Cooper, an eminent eye-surgeon (d. 1878). Cooper's mistress Anne Julia Pearson bore him a daughter, Ada Nemesis, who married John Galsworthy's cousin Arthur. Ada was not happy in this marriage and entered into a long affair with John, whom she eventually married. Irene in The Forsyte Saga is said to have been modelled on Ada.

This cast-iron birdbath, with Moorish influences, commemorates the Hines family who ran a foundry (est. 1820) in St Margaret's Street off St Benedict's Street. The collection of heads is said to represent family members.

One of the best known memorials consists of a tomb on which stands a fine bust sheltering beneath a canopy. It tells the story of John Barker (1837-1897), a circus proprietor who rose to prominence amongst the travelling showmen with his steam circus rides. When setting up the Easter Fair, Barker was fatally crushed between two wagons, in Tombland according to one source, in the Cattlemarket according to another.

John Barker, steam circus proprietor

Both may be right. Until the seventeenth century the annual Tombland Fair was held on the Thursday before Easter. For most of the twentieth century, however, the Tombland Fair was held, not outside the cathedral, but in spaces around the castle where livestock markets were held, such as Cattlemarket Street.

The Rosary is a microcosm of mercantile Norwich in the Victorian era, where you will encounter figures whose works can still be seen around the city. Robert Tillyard, for instance, ran a leather-currying business that evolved into Tillyard and Howlett's (later Howlett and White's) shoe factory that succeeded the moribund weaving industry in becoming the city's major employer. For centuries, Norwich weavers had worked at home on hand looms and visitors expressed surprise at the lack of large weaving rooms. In the event, Norwich weavers were eventually priced out of the market by the large power mills of Lancashire and the West Riding of Yorkshire. Somewhat ironically, shoe-making, based on the same pattern of outwork employed by the city's journeymen weavers, did manage to adapt to industrial-scale manufacture and it was Edward Boardman who designed shoe factories, like Haldinstein and Bally's on Queen's Street. He was also the architect of Howlett and White's shoe factory in Colegate, which became the largest in the country, employing nearly 2000 workers.

When I visited the cemetery in 2017 I found a monument to the city's once pre-eminent weaving trade partly obscured by the undergrowth. The lettering on the large obelisk was indistinct but this was surely dedicated to William Stark, the master dyer who could stain bombazine the deep black required for Victorian mourning. He also came up with a formula for dyeing wool and silk shawls a uniform Norwich Red that turned the Wensum the colour of blood when the vats were emptied from his works adjacent to the Duke's Palace Bridge. The river had been polluted like this for generations, long before the bridge was built; in 1681 Thomas Baskerville described the ducal palace as being 'seated in a dung-hole place ... with tradesmen's and

Stark's memorial obelisk

St John Maddermarket

earlier, in 1671, the diarist John Evelyn had written: 'I observed that most church yards (though some of them large enough) were filled up with earth, or rather the congestion of dead bodies one upon another, for want of earth, even to the very top of the walls, and some above the walls, so as the churches seemed to be built in pits.' Several examples of these overfilled graveyards can be seen around the city: including St George Tombland and St John Maddermarket (above)

dyers' houses, who foul the water by their constant washing and cleaning their cloth.'

In 1848-9 Norwich suffered a cholera epidemic and from 1855 the Home Secretary banned burial in the city's overflowing churchyards. Nearly two centuries

In 1856 the City established a public cemetery at Earlham and from the beginning it had space for unconsecrated as well as consecrated burial. The original Gothic-styled twin chapels for Anglican and Nonconformist burials were lost when the crematorium was built but Roman Catholic and Jewish mortuary chapels remain.

Possibly the most fascinating monument in the older nineteenth century section marks the grave of the horse dealer, John Abel (1800-1883).

While the versatile and prolific architect Edward Boardman is buried amongst his wealthy relatives in The Rosary his rival, George Skipper (1856-1948), rests in far less prepossessing style at Earlham. For his splashes of Victorian genius, Skipper's contribution to Norwich was compared by John Betjeman to Gaudi's in Barcelona. Yet, because failed investments thwarted his plans for retirement, the man whose grand projects had included the Royal Arcade and Norwich Union's Marble Hall was still grinding out plans – like those for the roads and drains of the Christchurch Road extension – aged 78. A member of the Plymouth Brethren, Skipper married three times, lived to 93, and is buried with his first wife.

It took some time for me to find George John Skipper's grave at Earlham Cemetery since much of the lead lettering had been lost from the headstone. In the sense that all things must fade this is fitting; it is, nevertheless, a sad testimony for a visionary whose creations still add sparkle to the city.

George Skipper and first wife, Earlham Cemetery

John Abel

By the eighteenth century Norwich had become a crowded city and those who had grown rich from the textile trade began to move out. In escaping to their country estates the wealthy marked their new social status but they also avoided the epidemics of cholera, smallpox and typhoid that swept the city. These estates formed a tidemark around the city, leaving in its wake an urban space that became colonised by hundreds of insanitary shanties.

Curious to find where the rich had fled I drew a circle around the city with a radius of an arbitrary 30-minute carriage ride. In doing this I found I was mapping mansions ringing Norwich that David Clarke had catalogued in *The Country Houses of Norfolk*. Expecting to see a diversity of trades I was surprised to find a circle of wealth maintained by a tight group of families who had been involved with weaving. 'Master weavers' who managed dozens of individual looms made money directly from the woollen trade; the more successful made money by handling funds and extending credit to their fellow weavers but the most successful – like the Gurneys and Harveys – formed country banks. Here is Burrell's Yard off Colegate, not far from from where Ives and the Harveys had their town houses.

Burrell's Yard off Colegate 1937 ©georgeplunkett.co.uk

Old Catton to the north offered a convenient escape for those who had business in Norwich-over-the-Water so that by the early 1900s this agricultural village had become known as 'the best residential suburb adjoining Norwich'. Gentrification had begun in the mid-1700s when wool merchant Robert Rogers (sheriff 1743, mayor 1758) built Catton Place. In 1816 this was to become the home of Samuel Bignold, son of the founder of Norwich Union.

Probably the most important house in the village was Catton Hall, built on a rise that afforded a faraway view of Norwich Cathedral that, at the time I published the blog post, was being challenged by the 20 or more

Catton 'The Firs', formerly Catton Place, in 1935. ©georgeplunkett.co.uk

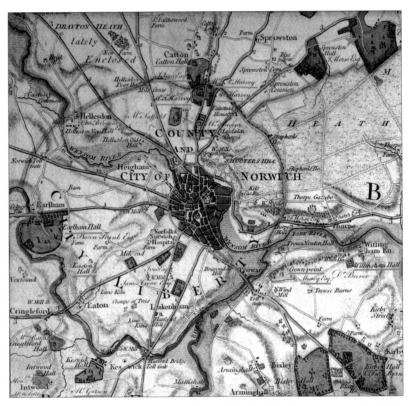

Faden's Map of Norfolk 1797. Permission of Andrew Macnair.

storeys proposed for a redeveloped Anglia Square. The wealthy worsted weaver Jeremiah Ives moved to this village from Number One Colegate where he lived within hailing distance of his relatives, the Harveys. Now he joined them in Catton as a fellow landowner. It isn't clear whether Ives purchased Catton Hall or whether it was inherited by his wife; either way, it was more than a little place in the country for in 1778 Ives gave Humphry Repton his first paid commission to transform the surrounding 45 hectares into Catton Park. In a small watercolour of the park Repton shows the steeple of Norwich Cathedral safely in the distance.

Faden's Map of Norfolk (1797) lists many of the houses that encircled the city, together with the names of many of the owners. Directly north of the city, at 12 o'clock, is Catton Hall around which are clustered the names of J Ives Esquire, Mr T Harvey, Mr R Harvey and Mr Harvey. At quarter past the hour is the village of Thorpe, where John Harvey lived at Thorpe Lodge (he was the textile merchant whose introduction of the Norwich Shawl temporarily revived the local weaving industry). Nearby, Whitlingham Hall is also associated with the Harveys.

Quarter past the hour on Faden's map is the name Crown Point and beneath this the words 'Money Esq' that could be the pseudonym of any Norwich banker except, as we saw in earlier chapters, the word can be traced to Major John Money who, despite his monicker, was not involved in finance. The Money family bought the estate in Whitlingham in the late seventeenth century and in 1784 John Money built a new house on the site. In 1861 the Crown Point estate was sold to Sir Robert Harvey, First Baronet, who engaged architect H E Coe, a pupil of Sir George Gilbert Scott, to build a new Elizabethan-style mansion with a large ornamental conservatory on a new site.

As one of the proprietors of what began as Hudson and Hatfield's Bank, Harvey built the grand Classically-styled Norwich Crown Bank on Agricultural Hall Plain, within sight of Gurneys (later, Barclays) Bank on the conjoined Bank Plain.

Harvey's Crown Bank on Bank Plain

Possibly to cover the expense of the new hall, Sir Robert had been speculating on the stock exchange. He incurred heavy losses that he tried to disguise as debts owed by fictitious customers and when the scandal broke in 1870 Harvey shot himself. Ironically, in view of their own financial uncertainty, Gurneys Bank bought the goodwill of the Crown Bank in order to quell local panic. The Crown Point Estate was sold to JJ Colman in 1872 and in 1955 the house became Whitlingham Hospital, now private apartments. Money's house was pulled down

by Sir Robert Harvey when he built Whitlingham Hall although the name 'Crown Point' lives on.

The name 'crown' associated with Harvey's bank building can be confused with its later use as the city's Head Post Office (until 1969) but the word refers to Major Money's Crown Point Hall named after Fort Crown Point where he had served in the American War of Independence.

Continuing the clockwise progression around the city on Faden's map, at 25 minutes to the hour is Keswick Hall beneath which is the name of Mr Gurney. Then we come to the yellow arrow above Cringleford that points to Thickthorn Hall (Gurney) just off the map. This is followed by 'Easton Hall' which appears to be a misprint for Eaton Hall (Easton Lodge was briefly owned by a Gurney but lies off the map further to the west). Earlham Hall is associated with the Gurneys, while Colney (New) Hall was bought by Hugh Gurney Barclay in 1887. What is surprising is how few families occupied major country houses in this first circle beyond the old city boundary.

The Harveys formed a dynasty of weavers and bankers, ten of whom were mayors of Norwich. The family had a considerable presence in Old Catton: Thomas Harvey built Catton House but there was also Robert Harvey at The Grange and Jeremiah Ives Harvey at Eastwood. Thomas Harvey (1748-1819) of Catton House maintained Harvey House on Colegate. He had married Ann Twiss, daughter of an English merchant from Rotterdam and formed a collection of Dutch old masters that would be studied by John Crome, a founding member of the Norwich Society of Artists who lived just off Colegate.

The Gurneys, too, had a major presence in Catton. In 1854, Catton Hall was bought by John Henry Gurney Senior who had inherited the bulk of the fortune accumulated by Hudson Gurney (1775-1864) of Keswick Hall (see below). The Gurneys were Quaker weavers who, through an extended cousinhood of alliances and partnerships, formed the country's largest banking network outside London. As financial intermediaries in the Norwich wool trade, John and Henry Gurney established Gurneys Norwich Bank in 1770. In 1778, Henry's son Bartlett inherited the bank that he ran with the help of two cousins, Richard and Joseph Gurney. Their city premises formerly belonged to a wine merchant whose cellars proved useful for housing the bank's safes that were protected by a mastiff and a man with a blunderbuss. Gurneys Bank was near the eponymous well on Redwell Plain, which would be renamed Bank Plain. In 1896, Gurneys Bank was to join 10 other private banks controlled by Quakers, to form Barclays Bank. Here is the Gurneys Bank building in the 1920s, rebadged as Barclays. Just after this photograph was taken it was replaced by the present red-brick structure built in the style of a grand Italian palazzo. The building may have changed but, astonishingly, the ornate lamp-post on the left occupies the same spot.

In the nineteenth century, the London branch of this Norwich bank became the world's greatest bill-discounting house, allowing a character in a Gilbert

Catton Hall in 1986. The distinctive dome of the Camellia House was removed in the war. © georgeplunkett.co.uk

and Sullivan operetta to sing, 'I became as rich as the Gurneys'. Influenced by what he had seen at the Great Exhibition held in the Crystal Palace, JH Gurney Senior extended Catton Hall with a cast-iron and glass Camellia House designed by Edward Boardman and manufactured in Boulton & Paul's Rose Lane Works in Norwich. The fine cupola was removed in World War Two to prevent enemy planes using it as a landmark on the way to RAF St Faith's (now Norwich Airport) and on to the city.

The former Gurneys, Birkbeck, Barclay and Buxton Bank on BankPlain Norwich, shown as Barclays Bank in the 1920s.
©Barclays Group Archives.

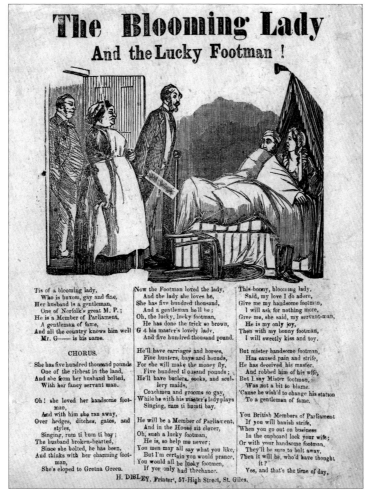

The lady and the footman. Courtesy of Norfolk County Council Library and Information Service

The bank in which John Henry Gurney Senior was a major shareholder (Overend, Gurney & Co) went bust in May 1866 with £11,000,000 liabilities. The bank's failure triggered an early Black Friday in the City and led to Gurney selling Catton Hall to his cousin, Samuel Gurney Buxton, a banker at Barclays. To compound his woes, Gurney's wife, Mary Jary, ran off with one of the grooms.

The bolting wife, Mary Jary Gurney, had come from Thickthorn Hall, a few miles south-west of Norwich at Hethersett. She had lived in this early nineteenth century house that came into the possession of Richard Hanbury Gurney when the owner defaulted on his mortgage. It stayed in the Gurney family until the 1930s when it was bought by Alan Rees Colman, director of Colmans and second son of Russell Colman of Crown Point.

Thickthorn Hall. Courtesy of Cathy Piccolo

It would appear that one family alone nearly succeeded in weaving a circle around the city for, in addition to Catton and Thickthorn, the Gurney dynasty owned country houses at Colney, Earlham, Easton, Keswick and Sprowston. Mid-sixteenth century Sprowston Hall (starred on Faden's map) was acquired in 1869 by John Gurney, the eldest son of John Gurney of Earlham Hall. Gurney employed Wymondham architect Thomas Jeckyll – he of the lost Pagoda in Chapelfield Gardens – to re-design it in Elizabethan Revival style. Jeckyll, however, could not resist inserting a gate in the fashionable Aesthetic Style that he championed.

In 1747, the worsted weaver Joseph Gurney came to Keswick Old Hall just south of the city. In 1811 the estate came to the fabulously wealthy Hudson Gurney who inherited brewing as well as banking money; six years later he had a new hall built in the Regency style. When Hudson Gurney died in 1864 his estate passed to his nephew John Henry Gurney of Earlham who had been tainted by the collapse of Overend, Gurney & Co Ltd. Much later, Keswick Hall was to become the new home

Jeckyll's japonaise gates at Sprowston Hall

of trainee teachers who had been displaced from their training college in Norwich's College Road when it was bombed during the Baedeker Raids of 1942. From 1948 until 1981 Keswick Hall was a teachers' training college; now it is a mixture of offices and flats.

Keswick Hall, south front, 1990. © georgeplunkett.co.uk

Earlham Hall, west of the city, is another Gurney residence associated latterly with education. For over a century the house was rented from the Bacon family during which time it was occupied by the banker John Gurney (1749-1809) and his family. Not all of his 13 children survived but Samuel, Daniel and Joseph John lived on to become bankers. Joseph John Gurney was also a Quaker minister and, like his sister Elizabeth Fry (née Gurney), was active in social and prison reform. The building now houses the UEA School of Law.

The city gates and walls disappeared around 1800 and over the next century and a half the once tightly corseted city began its slow but inevitable expansion. Campaigns of private terraced-housing occurred throughout the nineteenth century, followed in the twentieth by a prodigious programme of council-house building that overtook Eaton Hall and stopped just short of Earlham Hall. In the 1930s the outer ring road erratically tracked the new city limits and now, with the imminent

completion of an even more-enveloping orbital road, most of the banking circle will come within earshot of thundering traffic, something unimaginable to the merchants of the eighteenth and nineteenth centuries who sought rural isolation.

Earlham Hall, north front, 1938. © georgeplunkett.co.uk

While reading about Parson Woodforde's shopping expeditions to Norwich around 1800 I was struck by the modest scale of the stores he visited in the streets around the marketplace. This was still the age of the small shop run by, and generally occupied by, the shopkeeper and family, some of whom were the parson's personal friends. The market itself offered everyday provisions: meat and fish, fruit and veg but a few yards away, separated from the hurly burly of the market stalls, the genteel could stroll along the newly-paved Gentleman's Walk and window-shop for luxury goods. Shopping had become fashionable in its own right. Displays would be seen through windows made of multiple, small panes cut from sheets of hand-blown glass. None of those shops survive in the city. Instead there are signs of the large Victorian shops and department stores that replaced them, with their huge plate-glass windows.

Chamberlins

One of the largest Victorian stores around the marketplace was Chamberlins the Drapers at the junction of Guildhall Hill and Dove Street. At a time when Norwich had 124 small businesses listed as 'drapers', Chamberlins was on a different scale, selling a wide range of soft furnishings in several departments that ran the entire length of Dove Street. Chamberlins also had a furnishing department that stocked 'one of the largest assortments of carpets, linoleum, floor cloths and furniture to be sold in the Eastern Counties.' Now, instead of going from shop to shop in the cold and wet, the citizens of Norwich could graze through several departments in the warm and take refreshments without leaving the premises.

Henry Chamberlin founded the business in 1815. His descendants became members of the local establishment: Mayor, Sheriff and Deputy-Lieutenant of Norfolk. Some idea of the extent of their enterprise can be judged from the centre spread of this 1910 trade book. The store occupied much of the block from Pottergate at the rear

Chamberlins in King George V's silver jubilee year of 1935.
©georgeplunkett.co.uk

Two centre pages of 'Citizens of No Mean City', Jarrold & Sons 1910.

to Guildhall Hill. Top right, we see the modern factory built in Norwich-over-the-Water by AF Scott.

Chamberlins' store was a product of the Victorian era but its factory in Botolph Street, designed in 1903 by AF Scott, represented an excursion into modernism. The factory, which housed 800-1000 workers, was illuminated by electric lighting, proudly powered by a dynamo supplied by the Norwich firm, Laurence, Scott & Co. Here, Chamberlins made a variety of clothing for the police and railways but during World War I, when they turned to war production, their entire output of waterproof clothing was requisitioned by the Admiralty.

Sewing Room of Chamberlins' factory.
©Norfolk Industrial Archaeology Society and Philip Tolley.

Chamberlins Ladies' fire brigade.
Courtesy of Norfolk County Council Library and Information Service

In 1898, Chamberlins was devastated by a fire that started in the premises of Hurn's (est. 1812), 'the oldest rope, twine, sack and rotproof cover manufacturer in the Eastern Counties'. Hurn's rope-making factory, with its 200-yard-long ropewalk, was in Armes Street in the suburb of Heigham but the shop where the fire started was in Dove Street at the corner with Pottergate. The new fire engine station was sited not far very away, in a yard off Pottergate, but it would not be open for another month. Despite the efforts of the municipal fire team, aided by two brigades from local breweries, the entire Dove Street side of Chamberlins was destroyed along with their neighbour, the Norwich Public Library.

As a result of this disaster, water hydrants and hose reels were installed at the end of each floor of Chamberlins' new building. Their Ladies' Fire Brigade is seen here during the First World War.

Chamberlins was sold to Marshall & Snelgrove in the 1950s. It was occupied most recently by a Tesco Metro that relocated in 2022.

Buntings

In 1860, Arthur Bunting set up a drapery in partnership with three Curl brothers at the corner of St Stephens Street and Rampant Horse Street, where Marks and Spencer stands today. The collaboration did not,

5 Buntings, St Stephens Corner and Rampant Horse Street. From, The Gentleman's and Gentlewoman's Court Review, Jan. 22nd, 1909.

however, last the year and the Curl brothers set up on the opposite side of Rampant Horse Street where a department store was built for Debenhams after World War Two.

As drapers, Buntings sold costumes, lace, millinery, costumes, mantles (sleeveless cloaks worn over outer garments), collars, yokes, frills, ruffles. Like Chamberlins, they had a furnishing department and a tea room. They also boasted 'what the Americans call the mail order business ... (with) the aid of well-got-up catalogues.' Despite their motto of 'Latest, Cheapest, Best', Buntings weren't positioning themselves at the pile-'em-high end of the market for they had a Liberty Room in which Arthur Lasenby Liberty's achingly fashionable Arts and Crafts fabrics, which he sold in his Regent Street store, were offered to a provincial public.

Buntings' Liberty Room. From 'Citizens of No Mean City', Jarrold & Sons 1910.

By 1913 all this was replaced by a modern four-storey building in reinforced concrete, designed by local architect AF Scott. The new Buntings was the self-styled 'Store for All' where customers were soothed by an orchestral trio from midday to six o'clock daily. But on the night of 29th April 1942, German planes dropped incendiary bombs. Three stores on Rampant Horse Street suffered heavily: Buntings, FW Woolworth & Co next door, and Curl's over the road.

Marks & Spencer on St Stephens Plain

Buntings was saved from total destruction by the strength of its reinforced concrete skeleton. It arose from the wreckage minus the fourth storey and the corner cupola. In 1950 it was sold to Marks and Spencer. Its neighbour, Woolworths, was beyond repair as was Curl Brothers, and both were replaced with modern buildings.

Woolworths

I'm not including FW Woolworth & Co as one of the big department stores; it just happened to get itself tangled up with the history of two of the city's major stores on Rampant Horse Street. Woolworths was more of a five and dime store (or, in this country, threepenny and sixpenny). I remember Woolies in my home town as a place to buy 'weigh-out' roast cashews and pick 'n' mix sweets, and where a friend diminished himself by buying a cheaper Embassy cover version of a Beatles record. Below, is Norwich's Woolworths building in George VI's coronation year of 1937, five years before the deadly Baedeker Raid. While the gutted building was being replaced on this site in Rampant Horse Street the staff were sent to work in the Magdalen Street branch of Woolworths – a medieval building now occupied by Spice Valley. The modernist post-war building would be absorbed in 2002 by Marks and Spencer, whose original cupola can be seen, far left.

Woolworths on Rampant Horse Street 1937 ©georgeplunkett.co.uk

Curls

When the three Curl brothers parted company with Arthur Bunting they simply moved to the opposite side of Rampant Horse Street to a range of buildings, including the old Rampant Horse Hotel that had been known as far back as the thirteenth century as The Ramping Horse. What had been the inn's billiard room became the Curl brothers' Outfits Department.

A fire insurance map provided by Norwich Union reveals that in 1894 Curls occupied only part of Rampant Horse Street; they shared that side of the block with Green's the Outfitters, while the prime corner site at the junction with Red Lion Street was occupied by the hardware store of Colman & Co. This neo-Gothic building, with a distinctive clock tower and tall pyramidal roof, was to become the first Woolworth's store on Rampant Horse Street; in 1929 the business moved to the other side of the street.

Like their competitors across the road, Curls were drapers and in addition to departments for china, glassware, wallpaper and furniture they offered their female customers a millinery department (hats), costumes and material for dressmaking. This was a large enterprise supported by over 500 staff, including those at the factory in Pottergate. By the end of the nineteenth century, Curls had begun to modernise their premises and the Rampant Horse Street facade took on a unified appearance. In the year of Queen Victoria's Diamond

Curls' Rampant Horse St facade. 1897 © Norfolk Industrial Archaeology Society

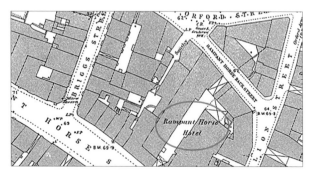

Curls took over the Rampant Horse Inn. © Ordnance Survey 1884

Jubilee they could proudly claim that the decorations were illuminated with 11 Ediswan street lamps, 'each being 200 candlepower'. Then in 1902 the Curl brothers remodelled much of the shop and built a new extension along Orford Place to the rear.

Curls in 1942. Courtesy of Norfolk County Council Library and Information Service

Uneasily, for a city whose once thriving trade in woollen cloth was stifled by competition from the north, Curls had a Manchester Department – 'Manchester' being the name for cotton products like flannelette and shirt material. The victory of cotton over wool had been won decades earlier in northern power mills centred around that city. Since the Middle Ages, Norwich woollen and silk fabrics had been produced on hand looms in weaver's attics – literally a cottage industry – but lack of investment, the absence of coal and fast-flowing water, combined with the weavers' reluctance to work in factories meant that the Norwich textile trade failed to meet the industrial challenge. Lighter, printed cloth manufactured in 'Cottonopolis' was highly successful but this popularity was tainted by the knowledge that it depended on the labour of slaves who picked the cotton in the southern states of America and the West Indies.

The neighbourly competition between Curls and Buntings on St Stephens Plain was ended by a Baedeker raid on the night of the 29th of April, 1942. Both sides of Rampant Horse Street were devastated and for several years afterwards, the block that once was Curls was just a very large hole in the ground, used as a car park and a water cistern.

The Debenhams building 2021.

In a remarkable act of familial cooperation, the Jarrold family let Curls, to whom they were related by marriage, occupy the first floor of their own department store at the junction of London Street and Exchange Street. Curls then moved into property provided by Norwich Union for burnt-out businesses where they traded as 'Curls of Westlegate'. Here, they sold children's and ladies fashions, millinery and drapery while their furniture department remained at Exchange Street. Curls had to wait until 1956 for all departments to be reunited in the new store that had arisen on their bomb-damaged site. This steel-framed building, which Pevsner and Wilson thought rather too bland for its position, was designed by Wilfred Boning Scott(1858-1981), one of AF Scott's two sons who followed him into the business. In the 1960s the department store was sold to Debenhams although they continued trading as Curls until 1973. The future of the store is uncertain after the recent failure of the Debenhams business.

Garlands

Richard Ellery Garland, born in Stroud, opened his own store in London Street, Norwich, in 1862. At 15, Garland had been an apprentice draper in the London area. His Norwich store – The Great Blouse House – was to

GARLAND & SONS,
Dressmakers, Mantle Makers,
. Milliners .

LEADING DRAPERS.

Telephone No. 256 for all Departments.

GARLAND & SONS

MERCERS GARLAND & SONS

GARLANDS

GARLAND & SONS DRAPERS GARLAND SONS

GARLANDS

HIGHEST IN QUALITY.   Choice Furs.

THE GREAT BLOUSE HOUSE.

LOWEST IN PRICE.
Dainty Lingerie and Corsets.

13, 15 & 17, London Street, Norwich

From 'Citizens of No Mean City'. Pub; Jarrold & Sons 1910.

specialise in drapery but we see from this advertisement that Garlands were also dressmakers, mantle makers and milliners who sold choice furs, dainty lingerie and corsets.

By 1920 it had become a store with nearly 30 departments. The central bay of the London Street

facade was very much as it appeared in the early 1900s but the Little London Street facade and the corner had been modernised.

In 1970, a chip pan fire in the kitchens spread to destroy the store, taking almost 70 firefighters three hours to get the fire under control. Jarrold's pensioners can still remember being on the roof of the neighbouring Jarrolds Department Store, putting out sparks from the Garlands fire.

Garlands, 1973-1984, Habitat 1985-2011

Garlands was rebuilt in 1973 in a curvaceous modernist style, its forbidding upper storeys supported by a colonnade that provided covered access to the ground floor shops. In 1984 the store closed and reopened the following year as Habitat, which occupied the upper floor until its closure in 2011.

BONDS

Born in the Broadland village of Ludham in 1844, the twenty-five-year-old Robert Herne Bond started his business in Ber Street, Norwich, as a 'Cash Draper'. He sold the now familiar stock of mantles, blouse materials, furs, ribbons etc etc. Competition between department

R. H. BOND,

15-17-19-21-23, BER STREET, NORWICH,

CASH DRAPER,

Has the Largest Stock of **Millinery** in the Eastern Counties.

A SECTION OF MILLINERY SHOWROOMS.

BLOUSE & UNDERCLOTHING DEPARTMENT.

Departments :

Millinery	Lace	Blouse Materials	Furs
Blouse	Mantles	Gloves	Ribbons
Dress	Underclothing	Children's Outfitting	Hosiery

The Public are heartily invited to inspect our Extensive SHOWROOMS.

DRESS DEPARTMENT.

MANTLE & COSTUME SHOWROOM.

Household Linen. ——— Furnishing.

An Immense Variety of Goods in all Departments

AT THE LOWEST CASH PRICES.

RH Bond, cash draper of Ber Street. From 'Ciizens of No Mean City'. Pub: Jarrold & Sons 1910.

Bonds All Saints Green 1939. Air Raid precautions. © georgeplunkett.co.uk

stores for the female market must have been fierce in this small city and Bond differentiated himself from his rivals by claiming the largest stock of millinery in the eastern counties at the lowest cash prices. According to their advertisements, all the large drapers in the city focused on clothing for women and children so where did men obtain their clothes? Probably in tailor shops, of which Norwich had 83 in 1852.

In the late nineteenth century a Major Crow owned 2-3 cottages on All Saints Green that he restored and converted to the Thatched Assembly Rooms. In 1915 it opened as The Thatched cinema before becoming Robert Bond's ballroom and furnishing hall. Bond now owned properties that extended from Ber Street through to All Saints Green.

Despite the solid brick wall built around Bonds in 1939 as an air raid precaution, the thatched department store was destroyed by incendiary bombs in June 1942. Immediately after the war, Robert Bond's third son J Owen Bond – who had worked with George Skipper – designed a new store for his father. This would be in the curvaceous Streamline Moderne style that emerged out of the pre-war Art Deco movement. In 1982 it began trading as part of the John Lewis Partnership.

John Lewis ('Bonds') 2021

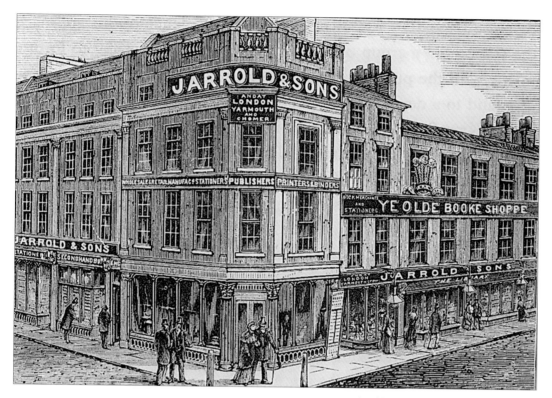

Jarrold & Sons ca 1890. Courtesy of Caroline Jarrold

JARROLDS

London Street, originally known as London Lane, was at one time known as Cockey Lane after the cockey or stream that ran beneath the road. This was a narrow medieval thoroughfare where pedestrians had to duck into doorways to avoid being crushed by carts. There had been talk about widening it since at least the late eighteenth century but this only happened in a piecemeal fashion: first in 1856 when the arrival of the railway created demand for better access to the market from Thorpe Station, then with Edward Boardman's scheme of 1876 at the south side, near the marketplace. By 1967, when London Street became the first pedestrianised street in the country, Jarrolds on the opposite side of the street was the only original business remaining.

Jarrolds began life in 1770, in Woodbridge, Suffolk where 25-year-old John Jarrold opened up as a 'Grocer, Linnen and Woollen-Draper' in the marketplace. In 1823 his son, also John Jarrold, came to Norwich. Young John announced in the Norwich Mercury that he and his eldest son John James were open for business in the city as 'Printers, Booksellers, Binders and Stationers'. This was on the Gentleman's Walk (south) side of London Street when it was known as Cockey Lane. In 1840, John Jarrold and his four sons moved their business across the street to the present location. Detached from the fierce competition between the other large stores who focussed on drapery and millinery, Jarrolds' main business was to remain the publishing and selling of books until the end of the century.

Jarrolds 2021

In 1896 George Skipper employed around 50 staff; his architectural practice had outgrown its Opie Street offices so Skipper designed a new building for himself at 7 London Street and became a neighbour to Jarrold & Sons. In 1903-5 the architect remodelled Jarrolds' London Street facade in a so-called 'free' Neo-Classical style that Pevsner and Wilson call Baroque; the overall effect being likened affectionately to a tiered wedding cake.

The curved corner bay would have looked even more ornate had it been topped off with the proposed copper cupola but Skipper was denied a trademark dome on his

London and Provincial Bank (currently the Ivy) further down London Street and was not to be satisfied here. The Exchange Street facade had to wait until 1923 for Skipper to complete the modernisation he had begun in London Street. At that time, the remainder of the block down to Bedford Street was occupied by the Corn Exchange (hence Exchange Street) but in 1964 Jarrolds bought the building and replaced it with a polite modern extension. The eastern-most wing on London Street is a seventeenth century timber-framed building with three gables that once belonged to the men's outfitters Dunn & Co but was absorbed into Jarrolds in 2004.

AF SCOTT, ARCHITECT: CONSERVATIVE OR PIONEER?

In writing about early twentieth century Norwich department stores I cited the architectural practice of Augustus Frederic Scott three times, more than local hero George Skipper, and even the prolific Boardman practice went unmentioned. Who was this architect whose design for Roberts' printing works was described in Pevsner's Architectural Guide as the most interesting factory building in Norwich and of European importance?

Scott was born in 1854 in the south Norfolk village of Rockland St Peter. His father, Jonathan Scott, was a Primitive Methodist preacher, one of the 'ranters' who favoured the original form of Methodism practiced by John Wesley.

AF Scott was educated at the old Commercial School in Norwich. This seems to have been the King Edward VI Middle School, established in St George's Street in 1862 as an offshoot to the King Edward VI School (Norwich School) in the cathedral precinct. In contrast to the more classical education offered by the main school the aim of the Commercial School was to prepare boys for industry and trade. The school was sited in the west range of the Blackfriars' cloisters that accommodated 200 pupils paying a tuition fee of four guineas per annum. Now it is part of Norwich University of the Arts.

Augustus Frederic Scott 1907. Christian Messenger Magazine.

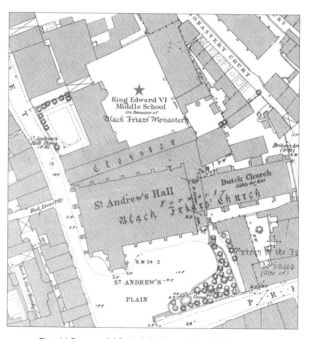

The old Commercial School, St George Street 1884. © Ordnance Survey

This complex of buildings comes down to us as the most complete medieval friary in England. Its survival can be attributed to the fact that in 1540, during the Dissolution, Mayor Augustine Steward bought the site for £233 on behalf of the city. Apart from a brief interlude when it was requisitioned as stables during Kett's Rebellion the priory has been in continuous municipal use: the chancel became the present Blackfriar's Hall while St Andrew's Hall became one of our most generous public spaces thanks to the Dominicans' original intention to design the nave as a large, uncluttered preaching hall.

In 1861 the architect to the trustees of Norwich School, James S Benest, began renovations in preparation for the opening of the Commercial School the following year. He faced the west elevation of the cloisters with polychrome brick and made additions in the Gothic Revival style, one of very few examples of its kind in the city.

West elevation of the old Commercial School

Scott was a man of strong beliefs: he would not allow his children to be vaccinated against smallpox. He was a life-long sabbatarian, a vegetarian on moral grounds and his abstinence from alcohol led him to

refuse invitations to design licensed premises. Along with high principle went irascibility. A letter from the Carron Foundry, who were casting windows for Scott, complained that they 'exceedingly regret to note the tone in which you write'. He is also said to have manhandled a woman who wanted to close a railway carriage window when he wanted it open. Scott also held back that portion of the rates used to support Anglican Schools. As a result, bailiffs would come to his house and take away his pictures but he always seems to have bought them back. In 1969 Scott's family gave one of his paintings to the Anglican cathedral. It is by Amelia Opie's husband, John Opie RA.

The Presentation of Christ in the Temple by John Opie RA. In Norwich Cathedral.

Scott prepared for his career as an architect by studying the practical side of the building trade with George Skipper's father, Robert, in East Dereham. He then spent two years with John Henry Brown who, according to Pevsner and Wilson, was one of the architects responsible for meddling with the west front of the Norwich Cathedral. After two years with the Liverpool Corporation, Scott began his own practice at 24 Castle Meadow. He was here from 1886 to 1927, for 17 years of which he was also Surveyor of Cromer. Scott was joined by his son Eric Wilfrid Bonning in 1910 and – when another son, Theodore Gilbert, joined around 1918 –the practice was restyled AF Scott & Sons. In 1927 the Scotts' moved their offices to 23 Tombland.

Augustus Frederic Scott was a distinctive figure in his 'wideawake' hat with a three and a half inch brim that, from the defensive tone of his description, seems to have drawn comments. 'My wide brimmed hat keeps off a certain amount of rain and sun and is of practical use. And moreover it suits me.' He is said to have been an enthusiastic cyclist although the adjective underplays the arduous journeys on which he embarked in the early days of cycling when roads were largely unmaintained and probably unmetalled. Scott claimed to have had the first bicycle in Norfolk fitted with pneumatic tyres, which would have been soon after 1888 when John Boyd Dunlop was awarded the patent for his invention. The architect cycled to Kings Lynn to catch the early train to Doncaster as well as cycling from Norwich to his office in Holborn Hall, London.

Augustus Frederic Scott, if he is known at all, is best known as the designer of numerous non-conformist chapels around East Anglia. Norma Virgoe compiled this non-exhaustive list:

West Acre (1887); Lessingham (1891); Garboldisham (1893); East Runton (1897); Postwick (1901); Lenwade (1905); Runhall (1906); Stokesby (1907); Billingford (1908); Fakenham (1908); Attleborough (1913); the Primitive Methodist (PM) chapel in Castle Street, Cambridge (1914) as well as Wesleyan chapels in Reepham (1891) and Cromer (1910). He also designed Baptist churches in Cromer (1901), Dereham Road, Norwich (1904) and Wymondham (1909). Scott designed Sunday Schools for the Primitive Methodists at at Lingwood (1878) and Queen's Road, Norwich (1887). He is also responsible for the Wymondham Board School (1894), the United Methodist mission hall in Ber Street, Norwich (1894-5), and Cromer cemetery chapel. Against

Tombland

the grain he designed two radically different buildings: a clothing factory in Botolph Street, Norwich (1903) and Bunting's Department Store, Norwich (1911).

The first in that list is at West Acre in north-west Norfolk, now home to the West Acre Theatre.

Primitive Methodist Jubilee Church 1887. Architect AF Scott

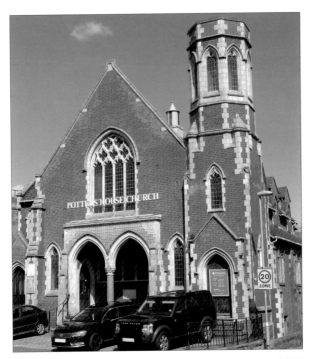

Dereham Road Baptist church 1901

to his father. The Jonathan Scott Memorial Church is perhaps Scott's finest church, built of red brick with stone imported from Ancaster in Lincolnshire – a more magnificent version of the Dereham Road church built the same year. The original plan had been even more ambitious but the proposed tower topped by a steeple was never built. Scott's connection with this church was severed in 1920, when he entered into a severe dispute with minister Percy Carden.

Jonathan Scott Memorial Hall (1901) Yarmouth Road

Before 1840, non-conformist chapels were often rectangular and plain with the long wall as the dominant facade but in the second half of the nineteenth century the short gable end became the focal point. Other denominations favoured Classical designs but up until World War I the Methodists seemed to prefer Gothic. Scott's designs showed an increasingly elaborate Gothicisation of the gable end as exemplified by the Baptist church on Dereham Road. Pevsner and Wilson's pithy entry reads: 'Hectic Gothic front of brick and stone'.

For 44 years, Augustus Scott's father, Reverend Jonathan Scott, tended his congregation in Thorpe Hamlet, a suburb to the east of Norwich. Too poor to have their own church his parishioners were, in 1876, allowed to pray in Blackfriar's Hall, once home to the city's Dutch Protestant community. Money was raised for a new Methodist church to be designed by Scott and dedicated

Most of Scott's buildings were in Norfolk but he did venture further afield with Primitive Methodist churches in Walberswick, Suffolk (1910), Cambridge (1914) and two Primitive Methodist churches in Lancashire (1904, 1908). These shared a strong family resemblance with his Norfolk buildings. Recurring motifs and combinations can be identified in Scott's gable end facades – notably the use of white terracotta tracery for the window over the entrance. This instant Gothic was obtained from

Red brick, Ancaster stone, Cosseyware diapering, granite columns

Gunton's brick yard in Costessey, a few miles west of Norwich. Letters in the Norfolk Record Office, in Scott's own hand, show him asking 'Mr Gunton, Cossey' for stop ends, mullions and string courses, describing pilasters and asking Gunton to 'proceed with the Cossey Ware in white for the chapel'. White clay dug, moulded and fired at the local brickyard had become an indispensable part of the architect's palette.

Scott designed a little curiosity in what is now known as the Golden Triangle – the Swedenborgian Church on Park Lane, Norwich. The Swedenborgian sect had had several homes in the city and settled on this street largely due to the efforts of James Spilling, editor of the Eastern Daily Press, who lived there. Spilling was a preacher and follower of Emanuel Swedenborg (theologian, scientist, philosopher and mystic) and

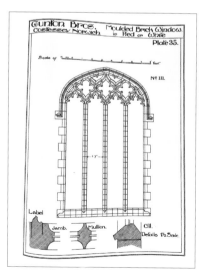

From the 1903 Gunton Bros catalogue

raised money to build the little church, which Scott designed in 1890. At one time Spilling preached in Glasgow where his homilies were presumably intelligible to his congregation yet back in Norwich his strong East Anglian pronunciation was considered a drawback. Eventually, the building on Park Lane was bought by The Church of Jesus Christ of Latter-Day Saints in the 1920s, and remained their Norwich chapel until 1963 when they built a new complex on Greenways, Eaton. The Park Lane building was sold to the Haymarket Brethren and then to the owner of the house next door, who uses it for concerts.

Swedenborgian Chapel, Park Lane, Norwich 1890

the arrival of the railways: from Norwich in 1877; the Midlands in 1887; and from Liverpool Street in 1897. The town's attraction had been boosted by 'Poppyland' columns in the Daily Telegraph in which Clement Scott (no relation) peddled a romanticised picture of the North Norfolk coast. To accommodate the influx of the middle classes seeking quaint fishing villages, poppy fields and ozone-laden air, AF Scott & Sons designed The Eversley Hotel. Rival George Skipper designed The

Grand Hotel, The Metropole and The Hotel de Paris, so he had form in the town, but the Scotts must have been incandescent when Skipper was invited to give their four-year-old Cliftonville Hotel an Arts & Crafts makeover. Skipper extended the hotel and updated the sea-facing facade. Like the Scotts, he made great use of decorative Cosseyware and here he added art nouveau touches carved by James Minns. Some of these details remain on the sea-facing facade although most of the red brick is now painted cream.

Cliftonville Hotel, Cromer.

Scott was Surveyor to Cromer Urban District Council and for a while ran his private practice from Church Street. In addition to the hotels, he designed Mutimer's department store, the old fire station, shops and houses. In 1909-10, he designed Cromer Methodist Church and Cromer Cemetery Chapel, which gave him the steeple denied him at the Scott Memorial Church in Thorpe. So, between them, Scott and Skipper applied the Victorian/Edwardian face on this seaside town.

Descending the hill into Cromer the visitor can't help but notice two very similar turreted houses providing the gateway to Cliff Avenue, one each side of the avenue at the junction with Norwich Road.

Fallonside (No 25 Cliff Avenue) and Kingswear (No 30)

Built between 1893 and 1905, Cliff Avenue is a late Victorian time capsule of fashionable housing for the affluent. Most houses display flashes of Queen Anne Revival although a decade or so after the pioneering Bedford Park in West London the style appears here as a more comfortable version described by architectural historian Marc Girouard as 'Queen Anne by the Seaside'. Scott designed houses in the street but there seems to be no firm evidence that he was responsible for the distinctive turreted gatehouses numbers 25 and 30.

While he was Surveyor of the Board (the predecessor to Cromer Urban District Council), Scott designed several private houses in Cliff Avenue. Some members of the board saw this as a conflict of interests but Scott replied that the board couldn't expect his full attention for £45 per annum. These houses for Cromer's well-to-do were, like Scott's churches, cosy, even formulaic: red brick with white-painted trim, bay windows, monumental chimneys, hanging tiles and verandas.

Some of the houses attributed to Scott in Cliff Avenue. Clockwise from top left: No.4 Marlborough House; No.6 Tudor House; No.24 Cliff Mansions; No.23 Ruth House; No.11 Kingsmead

It is hard to reconcile this side of his work with his excursions into the modern. The technology for reinforcing concrete with steel was developed in Europe

30-34 Botolph Street, built in 1903 as Chamberlins' clothing factory. Seen here in 1967.
© georgeplunkett.co.uk

and used in Britain in the 1890s. Designed in 1903 by Scott, Chamberlins' clothing factory (later, Roberts' print works) in Botolph Street was the first building in Norwich to be constructed with this material. Pevsner and Wilson thought this early example of European Functionalism to be the most interesting factory building in Norwich but, despite such plaudits, the factory was pulled down in 1967 to make way for Sovereign House and Her Majesty's Stationery Office on the ill-fated Anglia Square site.

Listed for 'its early contribution to the early development of the modern movement in England'

is the old Citroën garage in Kings Lynn, formerly the Building Material Company. Heritage England say this is possibly to a design by AF Scott. Constructed in 1908, this early example of a concrete-framed building boldly displays its structure without the need for disguise.

When Scott designed a new department store (1912) in Norwich for Arthur Bunting he employed a framework of reinforced concrete to which he attached a stone curtain-wall incongruously decorated with carved Adam swags. In 1942, German bombs devastated other buildings on St Stephens Plain, including Curls and Woolworths and though the non-structural walls of Buntings were blown out, its reinforced skeleton withstood the blast, remaining as the basis for rebuilding. Resurrected, but minus the third floor and its original corner cupola, it is now a branch of Marks & Spencer.

There are fleeting sightings of AF Scott in his latter years. One uncorroborated suggestion is that he was the architect of the Kiltie shoe factory in Norwich-over-the-Water; more certainly he was one of four local architects (including George Skipper) invited in the 1920s to design houses for the Mile Cross estate just north of the city, although it isn't known which bear his signature. When Augustus Frederic Scott died in 1936 he had not been involved in the practice for a number of years. His sons continued as A.F. Scott & Sons; in the 1950s Eric Scott designed the Debenhams building (now vacant) on Rampant Horse Street that arose on the bomb site where the old Ramping Horse Inn once stood. The business was amalgamated with Lambert & Innes in 1971, forming Lambert Scott & Innes who, now as LSI Architects, have offices at the Old Drill Hall on Cattlemarket Street.

Former Citroën garage 33-39 St James Street, Kings Lynn

Bunting's department store, 1942. Courtesy of Norfolk County Council Library and Information Service

JAMES MINNS, CARVER

In the latter part of the nineteenth century, before the rise of modernism and its rejection of unnecessary ornament, the architects George Skipper, Edward Boardman, Thomas Jeckyll and A.F. Scott all employed decoration on their buildings. For this they turned to a shy, jobbing craftsman – the 'carver' James Minns who was once called 'Norfolk's own Grinling Gibbons'.

James Benjamin Shingles Minns, son of Sarah Shingles and James William Minns, cabinetmaker, was born in Lakenham, Norwich, around New Year's Day 1825. The name 'Minns' is not uncommon in East Anglia and can be traced back to the Protestant Dutch 'Strangers' who imported it in the sixteenth century, when it was Mins. According to the 1841 census James had two sisters; he also had two brothers, both of whom shared their father's trade as cabinetmaker. Young James had woodworking in his blood.

James Minns. East Anglian Magazine vol 18, Part2

Westlegate 1939. The thatched building was formerly The Light Horseman.
©georgeplunkett.co.uk

Local historian E.C. LeGrice wrote that Minns lived in a house on Westlegate that was 'demolished – with several others – to make room for a modern block of shops' but an old shop in that cluster 'still remains ... under the very shadow of the tower of All Saints Church'. The only house to remain after Minns' house was pulled down was one of the city's rare thatched buildings, on one side of which was the church while its neighbours on the other side were demolished to make way for the Westlegate Tower. In the nineteenth century this thatched building was a public house, The Light Horseman. The horse on the pub's sign was, however, so poorly painted that locals named it The Barking Dicky, the regional name for a braying donkey, as in the old Norfolk rhyme: 'Matthew, Mark, Luke and John / Hold you the dicky bor while I gets on'.

After I published the original blog post, David Vincent sent this photograph of Westlegate in 1890, as Minns would have known it before the street widening.

Westlegate 1890, courtesy of David Vincent

The Ferry Boat Inn, 1936. ©georgeplunkett.co.uk

The national census provides no clue to when Minns lived in Westlegate. By 1851 he was listed as a 'visitor' in the house of a widow, dressmaker Frances Scales at 180 Kensington Place, near the junction of Queens Road and City Road but in 1858 Minns married Elizabeth Emily Thompson and, according to the 1861 census, was living at The Steam Packet public house. Confusingly, three Norwich pubs shared the name of The Steam Packet (a small boat regularly plying between ports) but a William John Shingles Thompson is listed as proprietor of The Steam Packet in King Street so it would appear that this is where James Minns was living with his Thompson in-laws. In the twentieth century, number 191 King Street was known as The Ferry Boat Inn.

Documents in the Norfolk Record Office indicate that in 1864 James Minns, wood and stone carver, bought two 'recently erected cottages, part of a row of eight', for £150 from the builder Edward Burton. Numbers 9 and 11 were in Arthur Street, a cul-de-sac off Mariner's Lane that formerly connected Ber Street on the high ridge, down the hill to King Street on the riverside. Minns had

moved up the hill from his in-laws' riverside pub. A note amongst Minns' conveyances in the Norfolk Record Office shows that in 1876, the Norwich and Norfolk Provident Permanent Benefit Building Society turned out not to be so durable and went into liquidation. Minns was allowed by the liquidator, Samuel Gulley, to redeem his mortgage for £20-8s-5d.

From 1851 to 1901 Minns described himself in public records with the plain no-nonsense English word 'carver', or 'carver in wood', 'wood carver' and 'wood and stone carver'. In 1881 there was a lapse when he used the Frenchified 'sculptor' but by 1891 and 1901 he was a 'carver' once more. This down-to-earth description of his profession was consistent with LeGrice's description of a 'shy and diffident woodcarver (who) had great difficulty in courteously excusing himself from being presented to his royal admirer, King Edward the Seventh'.

Minns' signature, Norfolk Record Office

Evidently, James Minns was no scholar, his only formal instruction being a little general training received at the old School of Art when he was a youth. An article in the Eastern Daily Press of 1904 confirmed, 'He was no laborious school-product.' It must have given him deep satisfaction, therefore, to have returned in his mid-sixties as Instructor in Wood Carving. This was about 1890, at a time when the School of Art consisted of an extra storey on the third floor of the Free Library on St Andrew's Street. From the start the accommodation on the upper floor proved unsatisfactory. Students were warned not to move about unnecessarily because the floor had dropped away so much that adjacent rooms could seen beneath the partition walls. Cracks in the chimney let the rain in, water closets were condemned, foul air pervaded the building – a problem not helped by students flushing modelling clay down the WCs.

Without a separate entrance and staircase to the top floor, access to the School of Art on the upper floor was awkward, leading to a demand by a student committee for a separate school of art. One of the petitioners was J.W. Minns. This was James' son John William who, like his father, became a Norwich Freeman in his twenties; John, too, described himself as 'carver'.

Despite his retiring nature James Minns was confident enough to instruct students in technical matters – after all, he had about 50 years of experience to pass on.

St Andrews Street Free Library in 1955. ©georgeplunkett.co.uk

He also had sufficient belief in the artistic merit of his work to successfully submit a carved panel to the Royal Academy's 1897 Summer Exhibition. The catalogue entry reads:

THE ROYAL ACADEMY EXHIBITORS
MINNS, JAMES … … … WOOD CARVER.
11, MARINER'S LANE, NORWICH
1897, 2017 A HAPPY FAMILY; PANEL, CARVED WOOD.

(11 Mariner's Lane may have been his workshop and 2017 the catalogue number).

The Royal Academy has no photograph of this entry and, having only seen his work in clay, I had no idea of the delicacy of his wood carving until I came across an example in LeGrice's essay on Minns in which he showed 'The Bullfinch panel'. LeGrice also mentioned that several Minns panels were in the possession of the Colman family. Several still are and I was kindly shown three panels of intricate, deeply undercut birds and foliage (although the curved glass posed problems for this amateur photographer). Amongst them was the superb bullfinch panel featured in LeGrice's article. Might this have been the 'happy family' exhibited at the Royal Academy?

The Bullfinch Panel, courtesy of James Colman

Minns' success at the Royal Academy was not isolated for, as the Eastern Daily Press noted in 1904, 'In competitions both at home and on the Continent he carried off some of the chief trophies of his time.' The carvings under glass are likely to represent his exhibition pieces. These high points of his artistic output contrasted with his bread-and-butter work at Gunton's brickyard in Old Costessey. Over decades he made moulds for decorative bricks that were turned out in their thousands. It was with one-off terracotta panels, as on St Bennet's – a Skipper-designed house in Cromer (1893) – that Minns was able to exercise his creativity.

Cosseyware panel by Minns. Private house, Cromer (1893).

On Skipper's former offices, London Street, Norwich.

James Minns' best known panels decorate the red brick building on London Street that was Skipper's office until 1946 and is now part of Jarrold Department Store. Architects were not allowed to advertise their practice but Skipper tested that rule when he commissioned Guntons of Costessey to carve six fired-clay panels celebrating his achievements. These were Skipper's glory years and if you look up at the panels on the red clay building you will see James Minns' depiction of the top-hatted architect set against a background of three of his major works: The Norfolk Daily Standard building in St Giles Street; Surrey House for Norwich Union; and Commercial Chambers in Red Lion Street.

In this tableau a top-hatted Skipper points to a shield presented by a bearded workman in a dust coat, with younger carvers to the rear. This senior craftsman, with flat cap and beard shares a similar profile with a figure identified as James Minns in a photograph of Gunton's workforce sent to me in 2016 by Costessey historian Peter Mann. The terracotta panels on the front of Skipper's office were being completed around the time (1904) that work was starting on another of Skipper's projects – remodelling the London Street facade of Jarrolds next door. James Minns died in 1904 of symptoms including 'senile decay', which carries the implication that at least some of his later carving might have been done by others, including Minns' son John. In a recent book on George Skipper (2020), however, Richard Barnes presents evidence from one of Skipper's surveyors that 'everyone in the office joined in the carving' (of the London Street panels). It seems unlikely that surveyors and draughtsmen carved the entire panels but this might explain the somewhat awkward depiction of Gunton's master carver who died that year.

Skipper didn't always work in clay. In his capacity as builder, George Gunton renovated the church at St Michael the Archangel, Booton, about six miles from Costessey. Minns carved the huge wooden angels whirring on high in the nave.

Carved angel by Minns. St Michael the Archangel, Booton.

James Minns' employment with Guntons was evidently flexible enough to allow him to work with local architects and designers in materials other than baked clay. He seems not to have produced much work in bronze although the figure of Saint Michael over the door at Booton church has been tentatively assigned to him. One specialist perceived that the sculptor was uncomfortable working with bronze.

Minns also worked with Thomas Jeckyll on the Norfolk Gates – an exhibition piece by the Norwich foundry of Barnard Bishop and Barnards (1862) that was presented as a wedding gift by the people of Norfolk to the Prince (later, King Edward VII) and Princess of Wales at Sandringham. Hand-wrought ironwork dominates but the piers and their base panels were cast and this is where Minns made his contribution that brought him to the attention of the future king. The cast-iron panel on the left shows a most elaborate version of the Norwich coat of arms supported by two armed angels (one missing a sword blade). The panel on the right is one of at least two wooden carvings that Minns made for the mould in which the coat of arms was cast.

Left: cast-iron panel from the 'Norwich' gates, courtesy of Sarah Cocke.
Right: wooden panel, ©hillhouse-antiques.co.uk

Archangel Michael, possibly by Minns

Minns carved the bull's head that is said to have inspired the trade mark on Colman's mustard tins.

Left: Bull's head by Minns ©E.C.LeGrice. Right: Colman's mustard tin.

Mantelpiece in the Old Library at Carrow House carved by James Minns (except the four small heads). Courtesy of Sam Johns.

James Minns also did much of the carving in the Colman's home at Carrow House. Helen Colman, daughter of Jeremiah James Colman and Caroline Cozens-Hardy reminisced, 'My Father and Mother returned to Carrow House on June 7th 1861 though it was still more or less in the hands of workmen ... but the wood carving in oak in the Library ... was for the most part done during the 'sixties ... it was nearly all carved locally, and much of it by James Minns.'

Dated 1862, the fireplace in the Old Library at Carrow House is richly carved with birds, flowers and foliage. The four human heads, however, were said by Helen Colman to be 'carved by someone from a distance'; i.e., not Minns.

The remodelling of Carrow House is thought to have been carried out by Edward Boardman (whose son was to marry into the Colman family) and he would have been familiar with James Minns. Indeed, a footnote on Boardman's plans for the 1891 renovation of the manor house at Catton specifically named the Minns family of carvers and not James Minns alone.

Although the Colman family were Nonconformist they supported church-going amongst their workers and donated a reredos of the Last Supper to St Andrew's

Trowse, which was only a short walk from Colman's Carrow Works. The panel is said to be 'a copy of an Italian masterpiece, carved by James Minns of Lakenham'. It was dedicated in 1905, a year after Minns died.

George Skipper's masterwork was Surrey House, headquarters of Norwich Union (now Aviva) in Surrey Street, and was completed in 1904. A 2008 conservation plan for Aviva states that H.H. Martyn & Co of Cheltenham, who specialised in woodwork and panelling, were assisted by James Minns of 11 Arthur Street, Norwich, 'including the carved figures over the

Figures above doorway in Norwich Union boardroom

main doorway.' The inclusion of Minns' correct address lends credibility although the mahogany carvings of female figures lolling on the pediment aren't the usual Minns territory.

More in keeping with the skilfully carved foliage displayed in Minns' bird tableaux are the baroque swags of fruit and flowers hanging on the mahogany panelling in the boardroom. These are highly reminiscent of the work of Grinling Gibbons' – King's Carver to Charles II. The five-petalled flowers are identical in both works shown below and it was hardly a stretch when Le Grice conferred the title of 'Norfolk's Grinling Gibbons' on Minns. On the other hand, reproductions of Grinling Gibbons carvings were also a speciality of Martyn's of Cheltenham so we await corroboration that James Minns was the actual carver.

The cause of James Minns' death on the 6th of August 1904 was given as cardiac syncope. The death certificate also mentions senile decay that, as we saw with the terracotta panels on Skipper's office, must cast a shadow over the authorship of work attributed to him in his latter years. The term 'senile decay' did not apply to normal ageing processes but described someone suffering from Alzheimer's disease, raising the possibility that others contributed work in the family name. James Benjamin Shingles Minns left £200 to his son John plus 'effects'. In his obituary the Eastern Daily Press wrote: 'There passed away this week in Norwich a brilliant practitioner of a delightful form of art. As a wood carver Mr Minns was in the utmost sense of that term a genius.'

Left: Surrey House (by author), Norwich.
Right: Grinling Gibbons at Hampton Court Palace (by Camster2, Creative Commons Licence)

WHEN NORWICH WAS THE CENTRE OF THE (NATURAL) WORLD

In the eighteenth and nineteenth centuries, naturalists collected plants and animals from all parts of the world and devised systems for classifying them into groups. The system proposed by the Swede, Carl Linnaeus, for identifying organisms was the basis for the one we use today. When Norwich-born James Edward Smith brought Linnaeus' own collection of dried plants to the city, Norwich became the magnet for scientists who wished to consult the Linnean standards.

Smith age 3 years 8 months, by Mrs Dawson Turner after a drawing by T Worlidge.

Sir James Edward Smith (artist unknown). Wikimedia Commons

James Edward Smith (1759-1828) was son of James Smith (1727-1795), a wealthy Norwich wool merchant. This was at a time when Norwich could still claim to be one of England's major cities, before mechanisation allowed the northern towns to dominate the textile trade. James Edward was a shy, delicate child who was taught at home, at 37 Gentleman's Way. His mother's love of plants may have stimulated his precocious love of botany.

His continuing botanical education was to be shaped, however, by the family's Unitarianism – a liberal religion that rejected certain dogmas of the established church. At that time the two English universities, Oxford and Cambridge, only offered botanical studies as part of a medical course since physicians were required to prepare drugs from medicinal plants. But such studies were closed to non-conformists like Smith since only those who subscribed to the 39 articles of faith of the Church of England could receive a degree. Against a rising tide of dissent – and by 1829 one in seven of Norwich adults were dissenters – those who could afford it had to be educated elsewhere, at dissenting colleges or in Scottish and Continental universities. So James Edward Smith went to Edinburgh and, rather prophetically, started his studies on the day that the famous Swedish naturalist, Carl Linnaeus, died.

The Enlightenment of the seventeenth and eighteenth centuries saw free-thinkers looking beyond the rigid views of the established church and embarking on a more tolerant examination of ideas through scientific enquiry and philosophical reasoning. This was also a period of great exploration, not only mapping the physical world but collecting as many examples of its flora and fauna as possible. After the gathering phase came the sifting stage in which naturalists tried to decipher the underlying plan. At Edinburgh, Smith was a student of Dr John Hope, who was one of the first to teach the system devised by Swedish naturalist Carl Linnaeus (1707-1778) for classifying plants and animals. Decades later, Charles Darwin (1809-1882), a fellow Unitarian, would also study medicine at Edinburgh where he was exposed to debate about creation and whether species were God-given (i.e., fixed) or changeable.

The Linnaean system of classification placed plants into groups based on the number and arrangement of their reproductive organs. The sexual basis of this system was not without controversy. The Director of the Botanical Gardens in St Petersburg, Johann Siegesbeck, called it 'loathsome harlotry' for which Linnaeus' revenge was to give the name *siegesbeckia* to a small, useless weed. (Later, Smith was cautioned not to copy Linnaeus' foul use of 'scrotiforme' and 'genitalia'.)

The original Linnean system based solely on the arrangement of sexual organs was imperfect but two key parts survive in the improved version used today. The first was Linnaeus' method of placing organisms into hierarchical groups based on shared similarities, from kingdom down through class, order, genus, species (other groups were added later). The second survival was his binomial system in which the two names – genus and species – were sufficient to identify a plant or animal. Before this, plants were referred to by long, imprecise Latin descriptions whereas the binomial system could tie down a specific plant. For example, there are many roses in the genus Rosa but addition

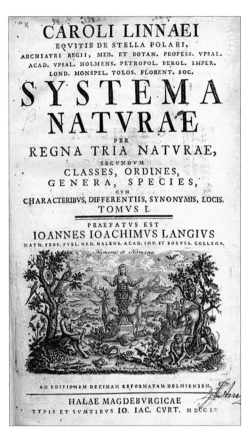

Systema Naturae by Carl Linnaeus, 10th edition. Wikimedia Commons

of the specific or species name *canina* distinguishes the dog rose (*Rosa canina*) from the red rose (*Rosa rubra*). Classification into hierarchical groups and the relatedness of species can be seen as an important precursor to Darwin whose Tree of Life added an extra dimension by showing that species were not fixed at the time of the Creation but mutable, evolving over time through the process of natural selection.

Linnaeus died in 1778; his son Carl inherited his father's collections and when he died only five years later they were offered to the President of the Royal Society, Sir Joseph Banks (1743-1820), who had befriended Smith in London. The Empress of Russia had tried to buy the collections as had the King of Sweden who, in a rather apocryphal story, is said to have sent a frigate to intercept them.

By RJ Thornton © The Linnean Society

Banks could not afford the 1000 guineas himself but persuaded Smith to borrow the money from his wealthy father and so James Edward Smith became possessor of Linnaeus' 3000 books and 26 cases of plants and insects. Smith was rewarded by being fast-tracked to fellowship of the Royal Society within two years. Three years later he founded the Linnean Society of London, remaining President for the rest of his life

But metropolitan life did not agree with Smith so he returned to Norwich for nine months each year. Ill health is often quoted as a reason but he was known to be fed up with the 'envy and backbiting of London life'. In 1796 he married a Lowestoft woman, the letter writer and literary editor, Pleasance Reeve. When she was 24, Lady Reeve was painted as a gypsy by the fashionable portraitist John Opie RA, the husband of Amelia Opie. Smith's young wife was to live another 79 years.

Pleasance Smith as a gypsy, by John Opie RA.

Alice Liddell age 20, by Julia Margaret Cameron. Wikimedia Commons.

Pleasance, who was childless, was evidently close to her niece Lorena Liddell (née Reeve) who gave her daughter the middle name 'Pleasance' after her aunt. This child, Alice Pleasance Liddell, was of course the inspiration for Alice in Wonderland.

29 Surrey Street, centre.

One of Linnaeus herbarium cabinets © Linnean Society of London

When Smith married Pleasance, her father gave them the tall Georgian town house, 29 Surrey Street, Norwich, as a wedding present. As we saw in chapter 7, this was part of the Georgian terrace designed by Thomas Ivory who had also built the Octagon Chapel in Colegate where Amelia Opie once worshipped. The garden that had contained Smith's beloved plants was sold in 1939 to the Eastern Counties Bus Co. Number 29 itself was bomb damaged during World War Two and the two neighbouring houses replaced.

For as long as he lived in Norwich the house in Surrey Street, not the Linnean Society of London, was the private museum in which Smith housed the Linnean collection. This included Linnaeus' three herbarium cabinets arranged so that around 14000 specimens – plants dried on sheets of paper – could be easily referenced. These 'type specimens' were Linnaeus' own best representatives of a species and, when scientists from numerous countries were drawn to the city to consult the collection, Norwich could claim to be the centre of the natural world. In 1938, two of the cabinets returned to Sweden while the Linnean Society of London retained the other plus all contents.

Smith maintained a prodigious output. Between 1790 and 1823 he published 36 volumes of *English Botany*. The series, which was issued by subscription, contained over 2,500 hand-coloured plates by illustrator James Sowerby; indeed, the work was sometimes called Sowerby's Botany because Smith – unsure about being associated with a popular illustrated work in English – left his name off the first edition. The John Innes Centre's Special Collection on the outskirts of Norwich contains a copy of Smith's English Flora with this illustration of a Lady's Slipper Orchid.

Smith also wrote *Flora Brittanica* (1800-1804) and *The*

Lady's Slipper Orchid from English Flora.
Courtesy of John Innes Foundation Collection of Rare Botanical Books.

Frontispiece of Flora Graeca.
Courtesy of John Innes Foundation Collection of Rare Botanical Books

English Flora (1824-1828). At the time of his death Smith had also edited eight and half of the 12 volumes of John Sibthorp's survey of Greek flowers, _Flora Graeca_ – a beautiful publication, each with 100 plates illustrated by Ferdinand Bauer (the final volume by Sowerby having 66 plates).

At one time, Smith instructed Queen Charlotte, the wife of King George III, and her daughters. He taught them the elements of Botany and Zoology but this relationship was cut short after he criticised the French court and discussed the republican Jean-Jacques Rousseau whose ideas had paved the way for the French Revolution: 'Man is born free, and he is everywhere in chains'. The dissenting mind once again confronted the establishment when Smith tried unsuccessfully to become Professor of Botany at Cambridge University.

His non-conformity, support for the abolition of slavery and of Greek independence, had not helped his cause.

Perhaps surprisingly, Smith did not bequeath his collections to the society he had founded and of which he had been president for life. Instead, he left instructions that they were to be sold as one lot to a public or corporate body, causing The Linnean Society to purchase the very reason for their existence for the vast amount of £3150 – a sum that took them over 40 years to pay off.

There is a memorial plaque to Sir James Edward Smith on the north side of the nave in St Peter Mancroft, Norwich, but his body was interred in his wife's family vault in the churchyard at St Margaret's Lowestoft.

There was a time when investigating the world around you could be a dangerous thing: think of Galileo's unpleasantness with the Inquisition for suggesting that the Earth might not be the centre of the Universe. On a more humble scale, a group of Norfolk botanists were at the forefront of systematic plant classification; they may have thought they were simply revealing God's plan but this was part of a larger movement from which the Theory of Evolution emerged.

The Father of Springtime' Robert Marsham FRS (1708-1797). Public domain.

Not long after the Galileo Affair, the Norwich physician Sir Thomas Browne (1605-82) was making systematic observations on the natural world, leading to the first attempt at listing Norfolk's birds. In the next century he would be followed by a network of local collectors who did the same for plants.

Robert Marsham (1708-97), son of a Norfolk landowner, made 'natural calendars' in which weather and temperature could be correlated with the arrival of birds and the emergence of plants. Over a 60 year period Marsham maintained tables of 'Indications of Spring', helping to establish the science of phenology, which deals with the seasonal and cyclic effects of climate on the natural world. Marsham had presented papers to the Royal Society on the cultivation of trees in poor soils; my wife planted trees for a living and so we made an excursion to Marsham's church in Stratton Strawless (gravelly soil, poor crops, no straw) to pay homage. By chance, this was where my favourite piece of Norwich School stained glass (the subject of my first blog post in 2015) is also situated, so we could both pay our respects.

Marsham shared this interest in botany and climate with his friend Benjamin Stillingfleet, born in Wood Norton, tutor to William Windham (1702-71) of Felbrigg Hall. When attending a women's literary discussion group in London, Stillingfleet is said to have been too poor to wear the black silk stockings of formal dress so came instead in his everyday blue worsted stockings. As a consequence, the literary group started in the 1750s, and presided over by Elizabeth Montagu – labelled 'the Queen of the Blues' some 200 years before Bessie Smith – became known as the Bluestocking Society; the word now a reminder of women who value a life of the mind, despite satirical attempts to undermine them.

Stillingfleet may have been the first in this country to use the classification system devised by Carl Linnaeus and, in his portrait by Zoffany, the former Norwich School pupil chose to be painted holding a copy of Linnaeus' *Species Plantarum*. Another early adopter

Breaking up of the Blue Stocking Club, by Thomas Rowlandson 1815. Public domain.

Benjamin Stillingfleet by Johann Zoffany, ca 1761. Public domain.

of the Linnean system was Stillingfleet's friend and neighbour in London, the apothecary William Hudson. However, in his foreword to Hudson's *Flora Anglica* (1762), Norwich-born Sir James Edward Smith makes it clear that this book was 'composed under the auspices and advice of Norfolk's Benjamin Stillingfleet'. Smith also acknowledged 'a small circle of experienced observers at Norwich' who propagated the principles of theoretical botany, attributing this rich microclimate to the Protestant refugees from the Low Countries who brought with them a love for the cultivation of flowers.

The principles of plant classification were vitally important to apothecaries who, as dispensers of herbal medicines, had professional reasons for the correct identification of plants. Hugh Rose (1707-1792), an apothecary of Tombland, collected the Linnean names of edible plants. Together with Reverend Henry Bryant, Rose produced a translation of Linnaeus's *Elements of Botany* to which they added an appendix on Norfolk and Suffolk plants. Both Rose and

Bryant were members of The Norwich Botanical Society, founded circa 1760.

The surgeon-apothecary, John Pitchford, came to Norwich in 1769. According to Gudrun Richardson in her essay, *'A Norfolk Network within the Royal Society'* (2012), Pitchford was 'last of a school of botanists of this city, among whom the writings and merits of Linnaeus were perhaps more early, or at least philosophically studied, than in any other part of Great Britain.' Sir James Edward Smith recorded that this Norwich and Norfolk circle was comprised of Rose, Bryant, Pitchford and Stillingfleet (supplemented by correspondence with Londoner Hudson), naming this small band as the founders of Linnean botany, not just in Norfolk, but in England.

Though not a Norwich man, nor a botanist primarily interested in flowering plants, the wealthy Yarmouth banker, Dawson Turner FRS (1775-1855), was to have a profound influence on this Norwich circle. Turner was a good friend of James Edward Smith and succeeded him as President of the Linnean Society. Turner was a man with wide-ranging interests and contacts and was centrally important in maintaining a web of scientists that extended beyond Norfolk. One of his correspondents was the eminent Welsh botanist Lewis Weston Dillwyn FRS (1778-1855), owner of the Cambrian Pottery and co-author of *'The Botanist's Guide through England and Wales'*.

The Turner bank house in Gt Yarmouth, pre-1840. Artist unknown, photographed by Stephen Bates. Courtesy of Great Yarmouth Local History and Archaeological Society.

Turner's wife Mary was also an ardent botanist, although 11 children hindered her full participation. She was a skilled artist and made engravings of drawings from her husband's collection, such as the portrait of James Edward Smith that we saw in the previous chapter. A year after Mary's death, Dawson Turner married the widow Rosamund Duff – a marriage

An apothecary using a pestle and mortar. Wellcome Collection.

deplored by his children. Turner forbade Rosamund's sister to visit his house but, after finding her hiding in a kitchen cupboard, discovered she had been secreted about the house for a fortnight. Imagine the uproar.

The friendship between Dawson Turner and JE Smith was close and, no doubt, some wry Victorian humour was being conveyed when Smith wrote to thank Turner for the loan of a rhinoceros horn that was being returned by Norwich School artist, John Sell Cotman. The blue plaque outside Bank House commemorates polymath Turner solely as a 'Distinguished Great Yarmouth Art Collector' although Turner may now be best remembered as the man who sponsored Cotman's painting expedition that produced *'Architectural Antiquities of Normandy'.*

Chateau Navarre, near Evreux, Normandy' ca 1830 by John Sell Cotman. Yale Center for British Art.

Turner studied non-flowering plants like algae, mosses, ferns and fungi that reproduce by spores instead of seeds. William Jackson Hooker, a young botanist born in Magdalen Street, Norwich, discovered a rare moss in a fir plantation in nearby Sprowston so Smith introduced him to Dawson Turner who was to employ Hooker's excellent draughtsmanship to illustrate his *Natural History of Fuci* (brown seaweed). Hooker became Director of the Royal Botanic Garden at Kew from 1840

to 1865. He married Turner's daughter Maria, and their son, Joseph Dalton Hooker, succeeded his father as Director of Kew (1865-1885).

JD Hooker was Charles Darwin's closest friend and confidant. Another of Darwin's inner circle was Professor John Stevens Henslow who had been his tutor at Cambridge and, as his life-long mentor, helped gain Darwin a place on HMS Beagle. Hooker was to complete the triangle by marrying Henslow's daughter.

Joseph Dalton Hooker age 80. Public domain.

Twenty years after the Beagle expedition of 1836, Darwin was still painstakingly amassing evidence to support his big idea that organisms born with natural variations, which allow them to adapt to environmental change, are more likely to survive and pass on those successful traits to offspring. That is, species are not fixed but evolve by accumulating favourable variations. Various arguments have been put forward for Darwin's tardiness: a parasitic disease contracted in South America; hypochondria; bereavement; religious scruple; or a determination to accumulate an irrefutable weight of evidence to support what he knew would be a controversial and revolutionary idea.

But before Darwin could publish his work the Welsh naturalist and explorer, Alfred Russel Wallace,

independently came up with the idea of natural selection and sent him a summary. Darwin admired Wallace's 20-page letter for concisely summarising what was largely his own line of thought and was understandably concerned that his own great work would now be 'forestalled'. In the event, Darwin's friends, JD Hooker and the geologist Charles Lyell, read a joint paper at the Linnean Society in which Darwin's and Russell's ideas were summarised. This was in 1858 and in the following year Darwin's 'On the Origin of Species' was published.

Charles Darwin ca 1854. Wikimedia Commons

Alfred Russel Wallace, artist unknown. Wikimedia Commons

Implicit in the Theory of Evolution is the idea that organisms living today have evolved over time rather than having been minted once-and-for-all on a single day: on Day Three of Creation for plants and Day Six for animals. Such a revolutionary concept presented a direct challenge to religious orthodoxy, prompting the historic Evolution Debate in Oxford, 1860. Bishop Wilberforce of Oxford (known as 'Soapy Sam' after Disraeli called his manner, unctuous, oleaginous, saponaceous) is said to have asked 'Darwin's bulldog' TH Huxley if he was descended from a monkey on his grandfather's or his grandmother's side. Huxley replied that he wouldn't be ashamed to have a monkey as an ancestor but would be ashamed to be related to a man who used his great gifts to obscure the truth. But in reporting back to Darwin, Hooker claims to have landed the more significant punches.

One early spring morning I followed the Hooker Trail in Halesworth, Suffolk. From the small museum I walked through the town, past Hooker House, ending up at the Memorial Garden & Arboretum. There I found examples of some of the plants named after the Hookers: *Inula hookeri, Crinodendrum hookerianum, Sarcococca hookeriana, Deutzia hookeriana* and *Rosa* 'Josephine Hooker' (JD Hooker's grand-daughter who lived to 103). On my return down the high street I bought the essential Hooker tea towel.

Not all of the Norwich circle were high-born or wealthy for although John Lindley (1799-1865) was educated at Norwich School his father was a nurseryman from nearby Catton. Lindley's ascent began when Hooker introduced him to the President of the Royal Society, Sir Joseph Banks, who employed Lindley in his herbarium.

The Hooker tea towel

John Lindley 1848, from 'Makers of British Botany'. Wikimedia Commons

The John Innes Centre and Sainsbury Laboratory. © John Fielding

Although he hadn't been to university Lindley became Professor of Botany in non-denominational University College where he insisted on teaching Botany as an independent subject, not as an adjunct to Medicine. As Secretary of the Royal Horticultural Society he revived its fortunes and if you visit the RHS headquarters in London you will have seen the Norwich man commemorated by the Lindley Library, which contains the largest collection of horticultural books in the world.

Botanical research continues in Norwich, home to the John Innes Centre. In 2000 this world-leading institute for plant science research took part in decoding, for the first time, a plant's genetic blueprint or genome. Now, the genomes of several hundred flowering plants have been published worldwide making it possible to line up their DNA sequences, to measure the extent of their relationship, and to estimate how far back in time they diverged – the molecular counterpart of Darwin's Tree of Life.

The blog post on which this chapter is based was written in January 2021 during the third national Covid lockdown. Perhaps it was the unlikely subject matter, or the fact that readers were trapped at home and only allowed to leave the home for exercise once a day, that resulted in this post being read by about 50% more than any other.

In these Covid times I cycle; along the celestial Unthank Road to the junction with Newmarket Road, then down the hill to Eaton and out to open countryside. Before the crossing is a house with two intriguing names carved in stone on the gate pillars. The first is badly spalled and its few remaining letters ... CRO ... would be unknowable except for a modern house-plate, Hillcroft. The letters carved into the adjacent gatepost are only slightly obscured and can easily be made out as Royal Norfolk Nurseries.

For several years I'd wondered about the clear, unbuilt-upon spaces on the early maps marked 'nursery ground' or 'garden ground'. The OS map of 1879-86 shows that the Royal Norfolk Nurseries occupied sites from the junction with Unthank Road (red) down the hill to Bluebell Road (blue) and a larger area between Bluebell Road and the river, now in the shadow of the A11 Eaton flyover (green).

Land in Eaton occupied by Royal Norfolk Nurseries. Ordnance Survey 1879-86.

Much of the land in the parish of Eaton, from the border with the Unthank estate in Mount Pleasant, Norwich, down to Eaton village, was owned by the Dean and Chapter of Norwich Cathedral. Much of the land in Eaton village itself was also owned by the church, with the exception a few oases, including 12 and 17 acre plots owned by the Corporation of Eaton.

The 1838 tithe map and accompanying apportionment record gives the name of landowners liable to pay church tithes and, within the two 'corporation' areas,

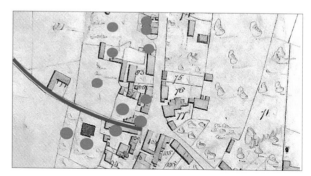

Plots owned by WC Ewing. Tithe map of Eaton 1838,
Courtesy of Norfolk Record Office

William Creasey Ewing (1787-1862) paid the tithe on most of the individual numbered plots.

His son, John William Ewing (1815-1868), inherited the land from his father and is listed as Nurseryman, Florist, Lime burner (and a lime pit is labelled on the map) and Seedsman. In 1851 the son is listed as living in The Old House, Church Lane, Eaton (formerly known as Shrublands), which he also inherited from his father. The house still stands. Prior to this census return, John William Ewing lived in Shepherd's House near Mackie's, the city's long-established and foremost plant nursery, founded in the 1700s on Ipswich Road.

John William Ewing. Courtesy of Vivien Humber

Between 1833 and 1840, John William Ewing and Frederick Mackie entered into a partnership, forming Mackie and Ewing's Nurseries, but in 1845 the

partnership was dissolved, leaving Mackie's to stand alone as the city's predominant nursery. Ewing evidently carried on for one of his invoices dated a year later announced that the Eaton Nursery was selling 'Forest & Fruit Trees, Flowering Shrubs etc' and, in smaller script, 'Garden & Agricultural Seeds, Dutch Bulbs, Russian Mats [woven from aquatic plants, used to protect trees and tender plants, exported via the Russian port of Archangel], Mushroom spawn etc.'

When he died, Ewing's Royal Norfolk Nurseries were inherited by his son, John Edward Ewing (1846-1933), but when John left Norwich in 1893/4 the business at Eaton was lost.

John William Ewing's headstone at St Peter's Church, Cringleford

In his *History of the Parish of Eaton* (1917), Norwich historian Walter Rye wrote that 'the chief trade of the village is now growing fruit trees and roses for the market'. He went on to mention other well known Eaton nurseries: the three rose nurseries of C Morse, E Morse and RG Morse and the 'old-established nursery of Mr

Morse, Ernest, born January 28th, 1872, at Eaton. Commenced business as a fruit grower at sixteen years of age, and ten years later extended his commercial enterprises by adding a Horticultural Department. Elected a member of the Norwich Board of Guardians in March, 1907. Takes a deep interest in the Congregational Church at Eaton, being the Sunday School Superintendent, and one of the Church Deacons.

Morse, Henry, born in 1858, at Eaton, near Norwich. Has been all his life interested in the Nursery business, and in 1902 commenced on his own account as a Nurseryman and Rose-grower at Eaton. He grows over 250 selected varieties of roses, having now forty thousand plants A member and Local Preacher of the Eaton Congregational Church.

Ernest and Henry Morse. From 'Citizens of No Mean City' (1910). Pub: Jarrold & Sons, Norwich.

basis. In 1759, this was taken over by the Aram family who were selling 'Scotch firs' in lots of a thousand for ten shillings. John Mackie joined the business in 1777 around the time the nursery moved to what, in its final days, would be known as the Daniels Road site.

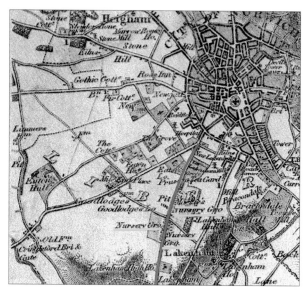

Mackie's nursery sites on Ipswich Road. Bryant's map 1826. Courtesy of Norfolk Record Office.

Hussey in the Mile End Road.' In 1910, Ernest Morse advertised himself in a trade book as a grower of fruit, cucumbers and grapes while his older brother Henry announced his 20 acres of rose bushes and fruit trees in the Westfield Nurseries, Eaton.

The Ewing and Morse businesses were dwarfed, however, by the industrial scale of Mackie's operations that made it one of the largest provincial nurseries in the country. Bryant's map of 1826 shows that Mackie's 100-acre site was situated around the crossroads where present-day Daniels Road intersects Ipswich Road (red line). The business can, however, be traced further back to John Baldrey's nursery in the city where, around 1750, he was selling plants and trees on a wholesale

Parson Woodforde knew Mackie. In his diary entry for the 13th of July 1781 he wrote: 'Mackay, Gardener at Norwich, called here (the parsonage at Weston Longville) this Even', and he walked over my garden with me and then went away. He told me how to preserve my Fruit Trees etc. from being injured for the future by the ants, which was to wash them well with soap sudds after our general washing, especially in the Winter.'

In an essay on the Norwich nurserymen, Louise Crawley – postgraduate researcher at UEA – described Mackie's site as being so extensive that clients were driven around it by carriage. Mackie's was to remain in the family for four generations until it was sold in 1859 when they emigrated to America.

Fifty years after Bryant's map the Ordnance Survey recorded that a portion of Mackie's Nursery at Lakenham had become the Townclose Nurseries. Later still, this was to be purchased by the Daniels brothers who sold the business to Notcutts in 1976. By superimposing modern roads on the nineteenth century map we can see how construction of the Daniels Road portion of the ring road in the 1930s (circled in red) bisected the Townclose Nurseries, to leave what would eventually become Notcutts garden centre on the south-western side of the new ring road. On the city side of Daniels Road the street names, Plantsman Close and Roseacre Close, remind us of the extent of Mackie's once huge enterprise.

In 1849 Mackie's ventured beyond the parish of Eaton when they bought The Bracondale Horticultural Establishment, situated in the crook between City Road and Bracondale. Patrons were welcome to visit the nurseries but orders could also be placed at Mackie's warehouses in Exchange Street where customers could buy seeds and catalogues.

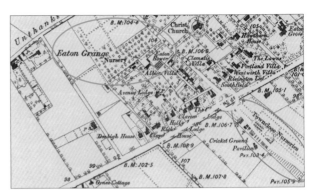

Daniels Road (circled red) bisected the Townclose Nurseries. Ordnance Survey 1883.

The Bracondale Horticultural Establishment can be glimpsed in a print from JJ Colman's photograph album: in the foreground is a plot with supporting canes while in the background there are heated glasshouses near TW Read's corn mill (1825-1900).

A trade card from around 1830 illustrates the surprising extent of the glasshouses that Mackie inherited when he bought the Bracondale Horticultural Establishment

Bracondale Windmill ca 1855. Courtesy of Norfolk County Council Library and Information Service

from JF Roe. Their hot-house produce included grapes, melons, 'forced fruits' and – most romantically foreign – the pineapple.

As a young boy, before I knew words like 'sybaritic', I visited Cardiff Castle and was shown a table with a hole through which a pot-grown vine would be placed for the Marquess of Bute's family to snip their own grapes as they dined. Nowadays, grapes are pretty low on the totem pole of self-indulgence (unless, of course, they are peeled for you) since they can be readily grown outdoors or in an unheated glasshouse. But in previous times the seriously rich would cultivate pineapples in hothouses, as much a show of wealth as a token of their hospitality. Indeed, from the sixteenth century onwards there was something of a pineapple mania amongst those who had heated glasshouses and staff to grow tender fruit and plants. Norfolk country estates may well have produced pineapples, but this would have been beyond the dreams of the villa-owning classes in the Norwich suburbs who looked instead to commercial nurseries like Mackie's to provide their hothouse products.

On a national basis, however, Mackie's reputation rested not with fancy fruit and bedding plants but with the quantity of their arboricultural stock. In 1849 they auctioned one million forest trees and in 1796 were able to send 60,000 trees to an estate in West Wales.

The journey from Norwich to Pembrokeshire required the trees to be carted to London then onwards by sea but such transportational hurdles would be largely overcome by the arrival of the railways. When trains did come to Norwich in the 1840s, Mackie's were able to offer 'instant arboretums' of 650 varieties of trees and shrubs for £35.

In his *History of the Parish of Eaton* (1917), Walter Rye mentions 'the old-established nursery of Hussey in the Mile End Road.' An advertisement from 1869 shows that Hussey & Son's Mile End Nursery on the north-west side of the Newmarket Road was, like its larger competitor (Mackie's), offering trees and roses – except Husseys sold their roses by the dozen.

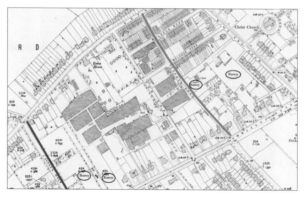

Ordnance Survey 1914. Mile End Rd (yellow); Leopold Rd (red); Judge's Walk (blue).

In 1885, Husseys occupied much of the area between Unthank(s) Road and Newmarket Road, stretching from the Mile End Road (in yellow on the 1914 OS map below) to what would become Leopold Road (in red). But, by the time of the 1914 Ordnance Survey, Husseys had sold much of this land for building terraced housing around Leopold Road. What had been open ground between Upton Road and Judge's Walk (in blue) was now occupied by glasshouses larger than terraced streets. These belonged to EO Adcock who had established a nursery producing plants on a prodigious scale. Meanwhile, Husseys had contracted and what

Adcock's Nursery ca 1904 ©Norfolk Industrial Archaeology Society 2014.

remained of their nursery was accessible through the entrance off Mile End Road.

Edward O. Adcock had begun his horticultural career as an amateur cucumber grower with eight glasshouses at a time when a dozen cucumbers commanded £1. To put this in perspective, in 1900 the pound was worth over a hundred times what it is today (although cucumbers are still 95% water). The reassuringly high price of this ingredient goes some way to explaining why cucumber sandwiches were the centrepiece of middle-class Victorian afternoon teas. As Jack said to Algernon in *'The Importance of being Earnest'*, 'Why cucumber sandwiches? Why such reckless extravagance in one so young?'

In an article eulogising Adcock as one of the *'Men Who Have Made Norwich'*, he is said to have had 125 glasshouses, each 120 feet long, totalling a quarter of a million square feet of glass. As well as cucumbers, Adcock grew chrysanthemums and, by selling 300,000 per annum, he claimed to be the largest grower in the world.

Twenty two acres were devoted to asparagus. Adcock also grew tomatoes in prodigious quantities: in one day his staff picked and packed over two tons of tomatoes to be dispatched by rail.

What fascinates is the sheer scale at which fruit, vegetables and flowers were produced in just one small part of Norwich. Adcock's were operating in the age

Packing tomatoes. ©Norfolk Industrial Archaeology Society 2014

of the train and could supply their produce around the country in reasonable time. On a less industrial scale, maps of nineteenth century Norwich give tantalising hints of allotments and other small nurseries such as: Cork's nursery ground; Allen's Nursery around Sigismund and Trafford roads in Lakenham; the nursery ground off Dereham Road; the Victoria Nursery in Peafields, Lakenham; George Lindley's nursery at Catton. Long before refrigerated transport and the concept of food miles it was this web of horticultural enterprises that, together with our farms and markets, fed Norwich.

PLANTSMAN CLOSE
CUL · DE · SAC

The previous post on Victorian plant nurseries concentrated within a single Norwich parish seems to have struck a chord in this city with a long history of horticulture. Not only was this my most-read post but the feedback was wonderfully informative. Personal reminiscences and comments brought the topic alive and I published them as a postscript.

As we saw in the previous chapter, the scale of some of the nurseries was astonishing: Adcock's glasshouses 'totall(ed) a quarter of a million square feet of glass'. One reader said she'd heard gardeners on Upton Road remarking on how much broken glass they keep digging up. Another, whose garden backs onto the site of Adcock's nursery, found a subterranean cistern in her garden.

On Twitter, Huw Sayer made the comparison between Adcock's nursery and the subject of an article in the Eastern Daily Press. More than a century after Adcock, a giant tomato glasshouse is being built just outside Norwich, using 'More glass than the Shard.' This low-carbon project is based at Crown Point, once the home of early balloonist Major John Money.

The only Victorian nursery to survive into the twenty-first century started as Mackie's whose grounds were so large that clients were driven around in carriages. After being bisected in the 1930s by the Daniels Road stretch of the ring road a portion of the original Townclose Nurseries lives on as Notcutts Garden Centre. This receipt from 1892 shows that in addition to their out-of-town seed grounds and nurseries around Newmarket and Ipswich Roads, Daniels Brothers had city centre warehouses in Exchange Street and Bedford Street.

Daniels Brothers' receipt, courtesy of Pamela Clark.

Tomato glasshouse at Crown Point. ©stepassociates

This part of the city, around what is now the north-west corner of Jarrolds Department Store, provided a shop window in the city for out-of-town nurseries. The location is perhaps not surprising since this was the site of the old Corn Exchange. As well as Daniels Brothers, William John Ewing of the Royal Norfolk Nurseries, Eaton, had a seed warehouse at 9 Exchange Street as early as 1854, while Mackie's and Stewart had a 'seed establishment' next door at numbers 10 and 11.

The arrow points to Bedford Street off Exchange Street. The Corn Exchange (1861) on the corner was replaced by an extension to Jarrolds Dept Store. © georgeplunkett.co.uk

Don Watson, who frequently commented on the blog posts, provided a link with the Daniels store around the corner: 'I remember Daniels' shop in Bedford Street because, being at school in Norwich, it became my job to buy the vegetable seeds there – much better quality than Bees Seeds from Woolworths (so I was told). That establishment was one of a few which still in the 1950s had only a beaten earth floor'. Dick Malt confirmed this recollection: 'Don Watson is quite right, the shop stood about opposite Little London Street and became The Granary when Daniels left. The facade is still the same as it was.' ... 'The Bedford St premises were where, at that time, seeds were cleaned and dressed for sale, both horticultural and agricultural. The cleaning floor was the topmost, under the roof. By the time I remember it, that aspect of the business had ceased and orders were packed there for posting out. There was a sack hoist from the ground floor and the warehouse manager's office on the first floor was connected by a speaking tube to the upper floor'.

Daniels Bros Seed Store in Bedford Street 1960s © Richard Malt

Simon Gooch said, 'I thought you might be interested in a little more information about The Granary in Bedford Street, filling in a bit of a missing link between Daniels seedsmen and Jarrolds taking over. My late father Michael Gooch (who was in partnership with my mother Sheila as M & S Gooch, Architects, in Norwich) converted the warehouse into a new shop for the owners Chapman & Pape in 1971-2. They called it The Granary, and at a time before Habitat or John Lewis had arrived in the city it was a bit of a mecca for good furniture and kitchenware. I have a couple of black & white photos

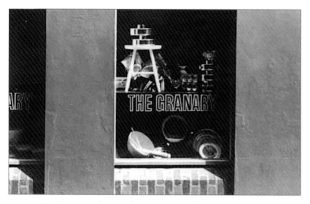

The Granary redesigned by M&S Gooch for Chapman & Pape c1972.
Photo Trevor Wood, courtesy of Simon Gooch

'My father was born in 1909, so was most likely apprenticed to the firm in about 1923. Some of the time he had to work on the firm's farm at Tunstead, near Coltishall, where seeds were grown ... He had to collect the keys to the Arcade from the Guildhall on his way to open up the shop. One sharp March morning he found the lock on the gates frozen up – a policeman thawed them out with a blow lamp'.

Dick sent me a printing plate advertising the Daniels Brothers' 'The Royal Norfolk Seed Establishment', which was their shop at 16-20 Exchange Street, shown here reversed for easier reading.

taken just after the shop opened, showing the smart typography of the name on one of the windows; the ground floor facade was painted a dark colour, I think purple (though being the Seventies it might have been chocolate brown). The interior's handsome pine beams and supports were exposed, and the wood and steel staircase inserted.' The building is now Jarrolds' modern furniture and design store and they retained the name, The Granary.

Dick Malt's account continues: 'This picture of Bedford St (previous but one) shows the shop in the 1960s. It had a long mahogany counter which had almost certainly come from the Arcade. My father, A.E. (Jim) Malt was the firm's manager and later managing director, having spent his working life in the horticultural and agricultural seed trades, beginning as an apprentice to Daniels. The shop was then in the Royal Arcade – I still have the keys!'

Jim Malt's keys to Daniels' shop in the Royal Arcade

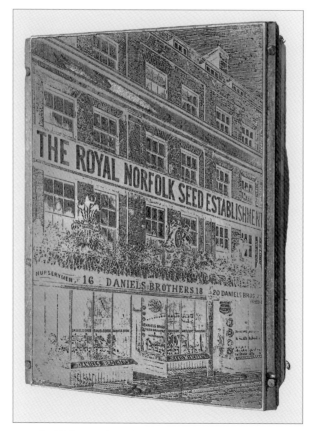

Daniels Bros seed establishment 16-20 Exchange Street © Richard Malt

The plate shows the building was originally five storeys high but numbers 16-20 are now much reduced. The discrepancy is explained by George Plunkett's photograph of the collapse in 1991 of the north-west end of the street.

Daniels Bros shop in Royal Arcade ca 1900. Courtesy of Stuart McPherson

Collapse of 16-20 Exchange Street © georgeplunkett.co.uk

Dick Malt suggested that Daniels may have moved to the Royal Arcade when it was opened in 1899. This early photograph (opposite) show that the business spanned several windows in the new arcade.

All this was to change in 1967 when the shop moved to the Daniels Road nursery site, now transformed into the new phenomenon – a Garden Centre.

On the day of the official opening of Notcutt's Garden Centre, Dick's father stands (back left) with the chairman Charles Daniels (top right). The two seated celebrities were Percy Thrower (the country's most famous gardener, a proto Monty Don) and Ted Moult (farmer, radio and TV personality).

Notcutts opening 1967. Courtesy of Richard Malt

Notcutts catalogue 1939-40.
Courtesy of Richard Malt

162

Norwich was slow to find its way into the industrial world. Before the slum clearances of the twentieth century, the city still had a timber frame – largely Tudor in appearance with Georgian contributions. At end of the nineteenth century the architect Edward Boardman introduced a glimpse of modernity with factories and offices built around steel frames with concrete floors, while George Skipper's more exuberant projects added sparkle. The contributions of these two Norwich titans survived well, helping to define the city's present-day character, but much of the fine texture from a century ago was built up by numerous smaller practitioners like Cecil Upcher.

Barnham Broom or Barnham Ryskys ss. Peter & Paul, and S. Michael with Bixton 1680		
Instituted	**Rectors**	**Patrons**
1764	P. Wodehouse	"
1795	J. D Ley	"
1813	Armine Wodehouse	"
1848	Alfred Wodehouse	"
1849	Edward Gurdon	"
1870	Maynard Wodehouse Currie	Earl of Kimberley
1873	Francis Raikes	"
1878	Arthur Charles Wodehouse Upcher	"
1887		

Upcher's father was rector of Barnham Broom. Norfolk. Photo: Barbara Worland

The name Upcher may be a corruption of Upshire in Essex yet census returns find it more frequently – though still scantly – in Norfolk. Cecil Upcher was born in 1884 in Barnham Broom, Norfolk, where his father, the Reverend Arthur Charles Wodehouse Upcher B.A., was the rector. The list of rectors and patrons inside Saints Peter and Paul is notable for the number of incumbents named Wodehouse after Sir John Woodhouse became patron in 1729. Patrons holding the advowson would have the right to nominate a candidate for the rectorship, thereby providing a living for a younger son. Note that Barnham Broom was also known as Barnham Ryskys in recognition of the rushes that grew profusely along the riverbank.

White's Directory described Reverend Upcher's home as 'a spacious residence with pleasant grounds near the church'. The 1911 census records that the Upchers lived in the rectory with a cook, a parlour maid, a house maid, a kitchen maid and a nurse. They lived well, in a manner appropriate to the descendants of Abbot and Charlotte Upcher who, in 1812, bought their estate near Upper Sheringham on the north-east Norfolk coast. They engaged John Adey Repton to design the Hall and Repton's father Humphry to reconfigure the landscape. Humphry Repton (b1752), was the foremost landscape designer of the late Georgian period but he died in March 1818, seven years after being badly injured in a carriage accident. In less than a year Abbot Upcher, would also die, aged 35, never to live in the hall he had commissioned.

Sheringham Park and Hall from Humphry Repton's Red Book © National Trust

Abbot's great grandson Cecil therefore came from Norfolk stock and it was as a Second Lieutenant of the 9th Battalion of the Norfolk Regiment that he served in the Great War.

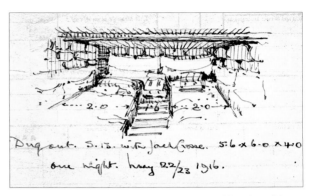

Second Lieutenant Cecil Upcher. Photo © Royal Norfolk Regimental Museum

Writing to his fiancée, Hilda Ward, he describes the conscripts as 'a top hole lot of men all true Norfolk men'. In his letters Upcher describes several of his billets, some of which he sketched. Since 1906, Upcher had been in practice in Norwich as an architect, specialising in church restoration. His professional training emerges in the sketch in which he measured the accommodation provided by a dugout: beneath a ceiling four feet high were two beds, six feet long and two feet wide, separated by an 18 inch gap. This and other temporary refuges were drawn with precision without revealing anything about the awfulness on the other side of the tin roof.

Upcher's letters convey the sense of the ironic, understated tone of the officer class – especially when wounded. 'Monday September 27th 10am [1915]. In the train. Here I am on my way to England I believe. I got a bullet through the fleshy part of my left thigh. No damage and as fit as a fiddle. Feeling a bit of a humbug to be leaving it all, but walking is rather a job at present. We had to take a Bosch position at 7am yesterday Sunday morning and I got bowled over with a lot of others I fear.' The voice will be familiar to readers of PG Wodehouse and the name Wodehouse, introduced into the family line by Upcher's grandmother, is inescapable here. When asked if he had taken part in the First World War, Bertie Wooster's manservant Jeeves replied, 'I dabbled in it to a certain extent, m'lord.' *(Ring for Jeeves,* 1953).

By mid-1916 Upcher was suffering from deep depression and was invalided out with shell shock. When he married Hilda the same year we see him holding a cane that seems too large for a swagger stick, suggesting he was still carrying an injury. Nevertheless, he returned to active service until the end of the war.

Cecil Upcher and Hilda Ward, Epsom, wedding day October 1916.
© Royal Norfolk Regimental Museum

Pulpit, All Saints Upper Sheringham

Upcher had been educated at Haileybury College, Herts before training at the Liverpool School of Architecture. Before the war, he was in partnership with Arthur John Lacey at number 6 Upper King Street Norwich. They specialised in church renovation and one of their last projects before the outbreak of war was the restoration of the ruinous St Martin, Overstrand.

After the war, in the church in Upper Sheringham that housed the Upcher family mausoleum, Cecil Upcher acknowledged men of the village killed in action, by designing the oak pulpit and the foliate reredos above the altar.

In memory of the men of the Norfolk Regiment who died in the Great War, Upcher designed a crescent of 12 alms houses for disabled soldiers. These are situated on the ring road near Mousehold Heath, marked by a memorial to the 6000 officers and men killed during the war.

Great War Memorial Cottages

Great War memorial (inset, Miller)

The medallion of Britannia at the top of this memorial is signed by HA Miller who collaborated with Upcher on a memorial in the cathedral. Herbert Miller (1880-1952), who trained at the Norwich School of Art, seems to have specialised in plaques with portrait roundels, including: Amelia Opie on Opie House in Castle Meadow; John Sell Cotman on Cotman House in St Martin-at-Palace Plain; George Borrow outside George Borrow House in Willow Lane; and the Baptist preacher Joseph Kinghorn on a house in Pottergate near the Grapes Hill underpass.

After the Second World War Upcher was to design housing for the wounded on an adjacent plot; this was a range of six cottages funded by the public via The Home Guard. Distinguished by their Dutch gables these cottages seem to belong to an earlier age; they may appear less generous than the two-storey accommodation provided by the Great War cottages but were designed for the disabled as single-storey bungalows in order to avoid difficulties with stairs.

Documents in the Norfolk Record Office confirm that Upcher's practice was involved in all aspects of restoration in churches around Norfolk. They were not, though, restricted to ecclesiastical work as can be seen in Princes Street where they restored Tudor buildings: number 24 in 1932 – stripping it back to its herringbone brick infill – and adjacent number 26, restored less vigorously in 1956.

Upcher and Carter at 24 Princes Street.

According to George Plunkett, the wooden lintel above the door of number 24 came from a house in Fyebridge Street, once home to Edmund Wood who was Sheriff in 1536 and Mayor in 1548. The repurposed spandrels retain the merchant mark of the Worshipful Company of Grocers (top right). And around 400 years later, Cecil Upcher and builder Robert Carter left their names carved on the door jambs of this house in Princes Street.

In the last years of the nineteenth century and into the twentieth century, when the city was expanding beyond the city walls, the Trafford estate in the parish of Lakenham was developed on land owned by Edward Southwell Trafford. In 1919 his son, WJ Trafford, extended the estate around Eleanor and Trafford Roads and in the early 1930s Upcher designed a church for the new community. As one of the few churches built in Norwich between the wars St Albans was very much in keeping with the surrounding detached villas – traditional but somehow comfortably modern.

In their *Buildings of England*, Pevsner and Wilson called the style, 'vaguely E.E.', although the church's rounded arches are clearly at odds with the lancets of Early English. By adopting a 'free' Norman style, Upcher may have been differentiating his new church from the work of the Gothic revivalists of the previous age. Prominent amongst the older generation of church builders in Norfolk was AF Scott who obtained his instant Gothic from the catalogues of Gunton's brickyard. Scott, incidentally, was still alive when St Albans was being built.

What the building *is* is vernacular. No imported stone here for its craftsmanship is celebrated in local materials drawn from Norfolk soil: unknapped flint with red-brick dressings.

West doorway, St Albans, Norwich

St Albans on Grove Walk and Eleanor Road, taken in 1938 © georgeplunkett.co.uk

Pevsner and Wilson described St Albans as being, 'In the Maufe succession,' forging a link with Sir Edward Brantwood Maufe (né Muff). Maufe's first major commission was Kelling Hall in north Norfolk, built to a butterfly plan. Following Norfolk's two other butterfly houses – Happisburgh Manor in 1900 (by Detmar Blow) and Voewood in 1903 (by ES Prior) – Kelling Hall was built in 1913 for the co-owner of the Shell Oil Company, Sir Henry Deterding. Like St Albans, Kelling Hall is clad in brick and local flint and, in making the connection with St Albans, Pevsner and Wilson are placing Upcher's church in the Arts & Crafts tradition.

Inside St Albans, the reinforced concrete ceiling in the chancel is a thing of beauty, predating the raw concrete of Brutalism by some 20 years – perhaps less a display of modernist leanings than an expression of the 'truth to materials' propagated by Pugin and Morris.

In 1955, in response to a competition by the Eastern Daily Press to provide a work of art above the altar, Lowestoft-born Jeffery Camp RA produced a large painting of Christ in Majesty. Christ floats above a panorama of the city as seen from St James Hill at the edge of Mousehold Heath – the vantage point from which Robert Kett's army fired down upon the city in 1549. A mixture of the city's landmarks, ancient and modern, point heavenwards: St Peter Mancroft; the City Hall completed in 1939; the Norman Cathedral and Castle; St John Catholic Cathedral ca 1900; and the tall chimney of what was once Caley's chocolate factory.

St Albans' reinforced concrete ceiling

Christ in Majesty by Jeffery Camp RA

The watergate or Pull's Ferry

Pull's Ferry by Cecil Upcher. Courtesy of Norfolk Record Office

Cecil Upcher is perhaps best known for his restoration of one of the city's most photographed landmarks – Pulls Ferry on the eastern boundary of Cathedral Close. Norwich Cathedral is faced with Caen limestone, each piece of which was shipped across the Channel in the eleventh century. The stone was transferred to low barges behind what was to become Old Barge Yard on King Street, allowing cargo to be delivered up the narrow canal connecting the Wensum to the stonemasons' yard inside the cathedral precinct. In the fifteenth century a flat-arched watergate was built over the canal and around 1780 the waterway itself was filled in.

The crossing from the opposite bank of the Wensum was known for most of its life as Sandling's Ferry. Sandling was superseded by John Pull who operated a pub here (Pull's Ferry Inn or Ferry House) from 1796 until his bankruptcy in 1841. The ferry continued to operate until 1943 although by the time that Upcher drew the watergate in 1928 the pub was already in ruin.

Cecil Upcher restored the house and watergate in 1948-9 and the Norfolk Record Office holds a small collection of photographs of the project. Wisely, they are sealed in plastic covers (I mention this to excuse the reflections on some of the photographs). The work was carried out by Robert Carter's firm who had previously collaborated with Upcher.

Work begins on the house. Courtesy of Norfolk Record Office

'C Upcher's room and armchair'. Courtesy of Norfolk Record Office

In memory of
CECIL UPCHER
ARCHITECT
Who practised in Norfolk
all his life
Born Barnham Broom 2nd Feb. 1884
Died Norwich 17th Sept. 1972

Memorial tablet to Cecil Upcher in Upper Sheringham.

After completion in 1949, the watergate itself became the headquarters of Norwich Girl Guides Association while the adjoining Ferry House became offices for Upcher's architectural practice. Plans show, however, that much of the space was dedicated to a two-storey flat. The largest room upstairs room was allocated to Upcher's nephew, James Fletcher-Watson, with whom he shared the practice, but the largest room on the ground floor was shown on the plans as Upcher's.

In the group photograph, taken in 1949, Cecil Upcher sits at the centre while standing to his right is James Fletcher-Watson (1913-2004) who trained as an architect under Edwin Lutyens, and is probably better known as one of the finest watercolourists of his generation.

Cecil Upcher died age 88 and is buried in All Saints Upper Sheringham.

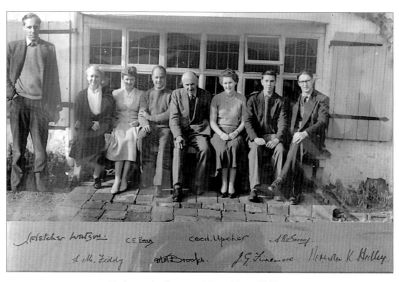

Upcher and colleagues at Ferry House 1949. Courtesy of Norfolk Record Office.

A seventeenth century visitor to Norwich, Thomas Fuller, was surprised at the amount of open ground within the walls of a thriving city but by the early twentieth century Norwich had burst its confines and green space was needed in the suburbs to counter-balance the Victorian terraces and the vast council estates that followed. One man planned the city's five extramural parks using the labour of men, many of whom were still unemployed after World War I.

From, South-East Prospect of the City of Norwich. Samuel and Nathaniel Buck 1741. Courtesy of Sanders of Oxford

In 1662, historian Fuller famously characterised Norwich as 'either a city in an orchard, or an orchard in a city, so equal are houses and trees blended in with it.' This sense of openness might seem at odds with what we read about the overcrowded yards or courts yet in the 1720s Daniel Defoe wrote along much the same lines: 'The walls of the city are reckoned three miles in circumference, taking in more ground than the city of London; but much of that ground lying open in pasture, fields and gardens.' The poorly-built dwellings thrown up to accommodate the influx of Protestant refugees from the Low Countries predate Fuller's visit by a hundred years so it would appear that while the city fathers turned a blind eye to overcrowding they evidently preserved the open green spaces.

Slum clearance had begun in the late nineteenth century but was far from complete by the time the city's soldiers returned from the First World War to their 'land fit for heroes'. Many ex-soldiers found themselves out of work; by 1921, the city had 7000 unemployed with another 1000 on short time and nearly 3000 men registered for relief work. It was against this background that Captain Arnold Edward Sandys-Winsch (1888 – 1964) applied for the job as Parks Superintendent.

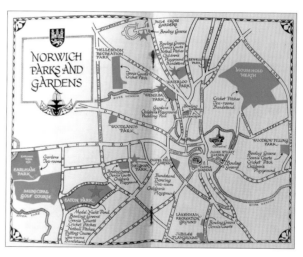

From, 'Norwich Parks: Summer Handbook' ca 1947. Sandys-Winsch's parks are starred.

Before the war Sandys-Winsch had trained with the well-known landscape architect and garden designer, Thomas Hayton Mawson, whose interest in town planning and public parks is likely to have played a part in gaining Sandys-Winsch the position. In 1900 Mawson had published The Art and Craft of Garden Making, linking his name to the Arts & Crafts approach to gardening pioneered by the partnership between gardener Gertrude Jekyll and architect Edwin Lutyens. Sandys-Winsch's designs for Norwich would emerge out of these formative influences.

When the captain was appointed in 1919, Norwich only had Chapelfield Gardens, Gildencroft, Sewell Park (funded by relatives of Anna Sewell, author Black Beauty) and the largely unreconstructed wilderness on Mousehold Heath (given to the citizens of Norwich by The Church in 1880). It was suggested to Sandys-Winsch that he could put the unemployed to work by making new parks.

In 1906, the council used funds provided by the Norwich Playing Fields and Open Spaces Society to buy 80 acres comprised of four large grazing fields between Eaton Hall and Earlham Hall. This area to the south-west of the city was at one time the site of the Royal Norfolk Agricultural Show; during World War One it served as a practice ground for trench warfare but between 1924 and 1928 Sandys-Winsch employed 103 men to transform it into Eaton Park. The scale bar on Sandys-Winsch's plan for the park indicates a plot more than a mile long.

Off to the right of his plan was a 'third field' near Bluebell Road, which was left as rough grass to accommodate circuses until after World War Two. Now it contains the pitch-and-putt golf course. Other recreational features included tennis courts, cricket squares, bowling greens and a model yacht pond. Eaton Park was the captain's prestige project and considerable effort went into the structural elements: mainly the radial plan of the large formal gardens and a centrepiece provided by quadrant pavilions surrounding a domed bandstand.

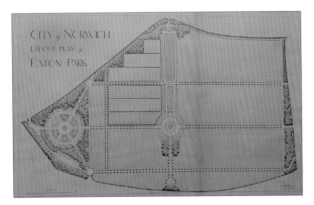

Sandys-Winsch's 1928 plan for Eaton Park. Courtesy of Norfolk Record Office

Sandys-Winsch (second left) in lock step with the Prince of Wales at opening of Eaton Park 1928. Credit: Eastern Daily Press

The park was opened in 1928 by Edward, Prince of Wales, with Captain Sandys-Winsch in close attendance.

At a time when finances were tight and few people had cars, 'holiday at home' was the slogan and parks enjoyed a popularity that is difficult to appreciate today. To help poor city-dwellers to enjoy open spaces, the Parks and Gardens Committee and the Norwich Electric

Eaton Park. Military band concert Whitsun 1932. © georgeplunkett.co.uk

Tramways Company arranged cheap fares for them to visit Eaton Park during band performances on Sunday afternoons.

The buildings in Eaton Park show a restrained Italianate classicism although there is said to be an Indian Mogul influence. The closest approximation to an Indian structure would be the domed bandstand, which can be traced through Mawson's designs to the dome-shaped 'chattri' pavilions used in Indian architecture and repeatedly employed by Lutyens in his designs for New Delhi.

One of the quadrant pavilions now houses the excellent Eaton Park café. When I wrote the blog post in 2019 they were advertising – with a nod to the park's creator – 'Sandys-Winsches', including one with a roasted vegetable and beetroot hummus filling. In the City Bookshop I came across a postwar tariff card that showed the refreshments available in Sandys-Winsch's time to be rather joyless. Probably printed in the tail of post-war austerity (World War Two), the no-frills tariff offered a 'set tea' of bread and butter with jam, a pastry and a pot of tea, enjoyed in clouds of cigarette smoke from Churchman (or other popular brands).

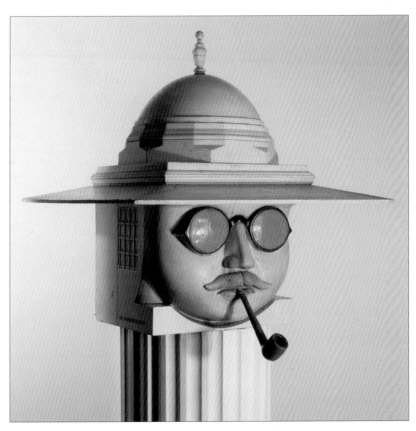

From the New Delhi office of Sir Edwin Lutyens 1912, based on a model of a 'chattri' roof.
©RIBA Collections

A dozen or so years earlier the pavilions had been used for darker purpose. In 1940, Britain was at war and the council was preparing trenches in parks and gardens across the city to afford some shelter against air attack. For Eaton Park the Air Raid Precautions Committee had drawn up plans to convert the pavilions to air raid mortuaries. North of the city, Waterloo Park was used as a temporary mortuary after two German bombers – a Dornier 17 and a Junkers 88 – dropped bombs during the first air raid in 1940. There was no warning siren; 27 were killed, including 10 at Boulton & Paul's Riverside Works and five women on Carrow Hill who had just clocked off at Colman's Carrow Works. By a curious twist a Dornier 17, which had been shot down over Duxford, was displayed at Eaton Park in 1940.

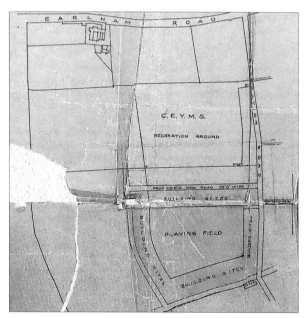

Skipper's proposed plan for Heigham Park. Courtesy of Norfolk Record Office ©Norfolk County Council

Less than a mile north-east of Eaton Park lies Heigham Park. Its survival amongst the blizzard of terraced house-building can again be attributed to the foresight of The Norwich Playing Fields and Open Spaces Society.

In what became the Golden Triangle, they had bought a large plot of land so that children at Crooks Place School (now Bignold) and the newly built Avenue Road School could take part in sports and recreation. In 1909 the mayor inaugurated Heigham Playing Fields by kicking off a soccer match between these schools. But by 1920, with encroaching suburbanisation, architect George Skipper was proposing to enclose half of the field with four terraces leaving the other half as a recreation ground for the Church of England Young Men's Society football team – the forerunner of The Canaries. In the event, the fourth (upper) side of the proposed building site (red) around Heigham Park was never built, leaving room for a generously wide road – The Avenues – to bisect the larger field and to allow traffic to join Avenue Road without too much of a dogleg.

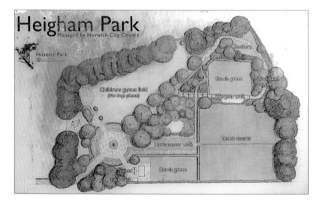

Heigham park sign

Opened in 1924, Heigham Park was the smallest of Sandys-Winsch's projects and the first 'modern' park opened in the city. Heigham Park had room for tennis courts, bowling green, floral beds and a general play area but lacked the large built structures that characterise Eaton Park. It does possess a timber pergola on stone pillars, which was one of Mawson's signature features.

The tennis courts at Heigham Park were once distinguished by wrought iron gates with railings

Reproduction Jeckyll sunflowers from Chapelfield Gardens

in the form of sunflowers designed in the 1870s by Wymondham's Thomas Jeckyll (no relation to gardener Gertrude). As we saw in an earlier chapter on the Chapel in the Fields, the sunflower became emblematic of the Aesthetic Movement that celebrated the impact of Japanese design upon Western art. Now, reproductions of these sunflowers form the gates at Eaton Park and Chapelfield Gardens.

In 1897 the Norwich Playing Fields and Open Spaces Association leased land from the Great Hospital Trust

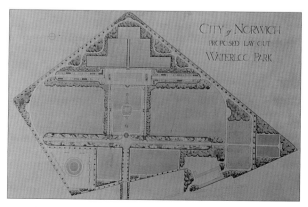

Sandys-Winsch's plan for Waterloo Park. Courtesy of Norfolk Record Office

that would become Waterloo Park in the north of the city. Originally named Catton Recreation Ground, Waterloo Park was redesigned by Sandys-Winsch and opened in 1933. This was his second largest project and was structurally more complex than Heigham Park. As at Eaton, this park provided for active recreation with grass tennis courts, football pitches, bowling greens and a children's playground. In addition were formal gardens – with the longest flower border in the city – pergola walks, a bandstand, a pavilion and again those colonnades.

One idea was to place a 'small central feature' at top centre of the pavilion. Proposals included a clock or sculpted heads of three of the city's worthies but during the renovations of 1998-2001, funded by the Heritage Lottery Fund, artist Alex Johanssen was commissioned to provide a sculpture of the three wise monkeys.

Wensum Park emerged out of an abandoned project to build a swimming pool and paddling pool on the banks of the River Wensum. After work ceased in 1910 the site became a refuse dump but in 1921, with a 40%

Wensum Park pavilion, steps and grassed over pool.

One of two pavilions in Mile Cross Gardens.

Newmarket Road

government grant, the council employed the workless to turn it into a garden park, which opened in 1925. Perhaps because of its gentle slope to the river, which made it unsuitable for playing fields, Sandys-Winsch decided to make this one of his less formal gardens. Unlike Heigham Park it did contain a building: a balustraded viewing terrace with a pavilion/shelter beneath. The steps running down from the pavilion once led to a circular pool with jets of water spouting from the perimeter but during the latter part of the twentieth century this was grassed over; the pool by the riverside also disappeared.

The last of the Sandys-Winsch's five gardens is at Mile Cross Gardens. In the 1920s Professor Adshead of Liverpool University designed a 'modern housing estate of quality' and from the outset the gardens were an integral part. Sandys-Winsch implemented the planned twin gardens, each an acre. While Eaton, Heigham, Waterloo and Wensum parks are Grade II* listed, Mile Cross Gardens are Grade II and, unlike the others,

did not receive Heritage Lottery funding in 2000. This secondary status is reflected in the dereliction of the two small pavilions and the loss of S-W's stone and timber pergolas (although vestigial bases remain).

Far more substantial is a pavilion that Sandys-Winsch designed at Sloughbottom Park but arguably his greatest contribution to the general wellbeing of Norwich's citizens are the 20,000 trees that he is reckoned to have planted around the city's roads. Planting trees along Class I and Class II roads was another unemployment scheme, funded in part by grants from the Ministry of Transport. Sandys-Winsch drew up the plans for Newmarket, Aylsham and Dereham Roads (all Class I) and Earlham Road (II) at a cost of £900, £408 of which was grant-aided. Now, nearly 100 years on, the captain's parks and trees add immeasurably to the quality of life in this city.

THE CITY HALL DOORS

The northern mill towns that put Norwich's centuries-old textile trade out of business celebrated their new prosperity with a Victorian campaign of civic building that passed our city by. By the time Norwich got around to replacing its medieval Guildhall in the 1930s the city had reinvented itself as a centre of light industry that could advertise its modernity, not with Town Hall Gothic or Georgian Classical, but with the clean lines of Scandinavian Art Deco. According to Pevsner and Wilson, this made Norwich City Hall 'the foremost English public building of between the wars'. The figurative roundels on its bronze doors provide a time capsule of how the city saw itself in this inter-war period.

In 1934, James Woodford had designed magnificent bronze doors for the Royal Institute of British Architects headquarters in London and was subsequently commissioned to design three pairs of bronze entrance doors for the proposed Norwich City Hall. Unveiled in October 1938 the 18 roundels – three per door – paid homage to history, trade and industry. The three pairs of doors are numbered 1-6, from the left, and the three roundels on each door are labelled A-C, downwards.

Roundel 1A. Bottling wine

Coleman & Co Ltd – not to be confused with Colman's of mustard fame, who took them over in 1968 – bottled wine that arrived in tankers from various European countries. From the 1880s Colemans also made Wincarnis, the name describing a mixture of fortified wine and carne, meat, from a time when this pick-me-up contained beef stock. Marking another proud first for Norwich, Coleman's were the earliest company in the UK to make wine-in-a-box. The factory on Westwick Street was destroyed by the Luftwaffe's incendiary bombs in 1942.

Woodford's images repeated in Chapelfield Mall.

All 18 of Woodford's designs – albeit in a simplified form shorn of Art Deco influence – can be seen around the top floor of Chapelfield Mall (2005).

Roundel 1B. Building the City Hall

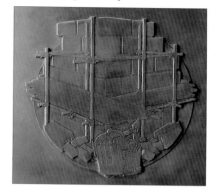

This illustrates building the base of the City Hall using blocks of stone with rusticated (set-back) edges. When buying a suit (a rare occurrence) in London the shop assistant told me that his grandfather, a master mason, travelled to Norwich each week to help build the City Hall.

Roundel 1C. The city's aeronautical industry

The city's largest industry of the time was centred around Boulton and Paul's engineering works on Riverside where they made aeroplane parts. B&P were used to making prefabricated structures like sheds and bungalows and in 1915 this led to them being awarded government contracts to build planes. By the end of that war the Sopwith Camel had become the country's most successful fighter (and, 50 years later, Snoopy's biplane of choice). Boulton & Paul are said to have made more Sopwith Camels than any other company.

Another contributor to the city's plane-building was the firm formed by Henry Trevor and his step-son John Page, registered at Upper King Street. Trevor, Page & Co. had made furniture since the 1850s and in the first war were contracted by the government to make wooden propellers. Trevor is perhaps best known locally for his transformation in the 1850s of a disused quarry on Earlham Road into the wonderful Plantation Garden.

Plane parts made at Riverside were assembled and tested on Mousehold Heath, which became Norwich Municipal Aerodrome in 1933. At the opening of the aerodrome in 1933, the Prince of Wales inspected a flight of the company's medium bomber, the Sidestrand – a twin engined biplane. In 1939, the Second World War was to begin and Boulton and Paul would contribute more advanced planes, including the Defiant with its four-gun dorsal turret.

At about the time that Woodward was designing the City Hall doors, Boulton and Paul's aeroplane

division moved to Wolverhampton leaving the former aerodrome to become the Heartsease housing estate. In 1971 the old RAF Bomber Command airfield at Horsham St Faith was redeveloped as Norwich Airport.

Roundel 2A. The filling of soda siphons.

Each of the big four Norwich breweries (Bullards; Youngs Crawshay & Youngs; Morgans; and Steward & Patteson) marketed their own soda siphons. Caleys also produced table waters from 1862, which were its main product until they began manufacturing chocolate bars and drinking chocolate some 20 years later. Caleys

Staff of Trevor, Page & Co with propellors, 1914-19.
Courtesy of Norfolk County Council Library and Information Service

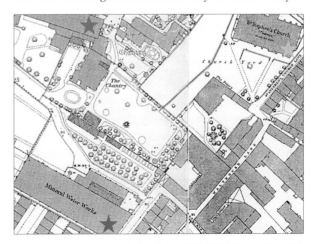

Caley's factory (red star). © Ordnance Survey 1885.

Fleur-de-Lys works in Chapelfield, which was destroyed in the Baedeker raids of 1942, was rebuilt only to be demolished in 2004 to make way for the Chapelfield shopping mall.

The Mineral Water Works can be seen on the 1885 Ordnance Survey map (red star). If you approach Chapelfield Mall by the path through St Stephen's churchyard, the church (yellow star) will be on the left and on one side and the High School (blue star) – now the Assembly Rooms – will be on the right. The site of the Fleur-de-Lys factory lies some 30 metres inside what is now the Theatre Street entrance to the mall.

Roundel 2B. The brewing industry.

Although Norwich is famed for its profusion of medieval churches, their number ('one for each week of the year') was dwarfed in the late nineteenth century by 655 licenced houses, grossly underestimated by the well-rehearsed 'and one for each day of the year'. Most of these were eventually brought under the umbrella of the big four Norwich breweries, all now gone: Bullards on Anchor Quay; Steward and Patteson's Pockthorpe Brewery on Barrack Street; Morgans at the Old King Street Brewery – the site redeveloped for housing as St Anne's Quarter; and Youngs Crawshay and Youngs on the site of Wensum Lodge Adult Education on King Street. Walking down King Street today you would

never know that this historic thoroughfare was once so characterful and home to two large breweries.

Roundel 2C: Making wire netting.

In 1844, Charles Barnard invented a machine for making wire netting based on weaving looms that would still have been a common sight and sound around the city. His Norfolk Iron Works was on the north side of the river, opposite Bullards' Anchor Quay Brewery. Trade magazines of the early 1900s would have shown very similar advertisements from two Norwich companies, both illustrating a roll of galvanized wire netting: one from Boulton & Paul Ltd and one from

Charles Barnard's wire netting machine at The Museum of Norwich

Barnard, Bishop and Barnards Ltd. The difference was that the latter emphasised they were 'Inventors and original makers', and cautioned clients 'against being misled into buying other so-called mixed mesh netting, which is in reality but two ordinary widths laced together.' Boulton & Paul's rebuttal was a laconic, 'lowest prices.' In 1903 B&P stocked over 700 miles of wire netting; by the start of World War Two they were producing 'Summerfeld' wire-netting track used to make temporary runways for aircraft.

Roundel 3A: Building the Castle

Assyrian-influenced flagpole base, probably by James Woodford.

If we had to guess the location of this scene from the scant clothing and hair styles alone we would be excused for placing these men somewhere between the Nile and the Tigris rather than cold old Norwich. This would at least be consistent with Assyrian-influenced designs for the two flagpole bases in the Memorial Gardens, which are attributed to James Woodford. Here, opposite the City Hall, the figures 'walk like an Egyptian': torso twisted, face in profile.

The roundel illustrates blocks of stone being hoisted up to a building with rounded Norman arches. However, something more efficient than the cranked windlass illustrated here would have been needed to lift large stone blocks (although the treadwheel only seems to have appeared in the mid-thirteenth century). Whatever

... it is stone that is being celebrated here, for there is none in this desert of flint and chalk, and to build both castle and cathedral the Norman conquerors imported their own facing stone at great expense from Caen in Normandy. Historian Sandy Heslop thought Norwich Castle was 'architecturally the most ambitious secular building in western Europe' and, as the only royal castle in Norfolk and Suffolk, this assertion of Norman power made Norwich the regional capital.

On this roundel we can just make out that the space beneath the rounded arch that frames the worker on the left is filled in with blocks of stone. Such blind arcading is a common decorative element in Norman architecture but the fact that a utilitarian building like the castle has external decoration at all is remarkable. As Pevsner and Wilson wrote in their *Buildings of England*, 'France e.g. has nothing to compare with Norwich'. Hurrah! By the

1830s the Castle had fallen into disrepair and the facing of ashlar from Caen was replaced by Bath stone.

Roundel 3B: Historical implements

The manufacture of fine woollen cloth (worsted) was almost certainly the city's major industry throughout the late middle ages and this roundel celebrates some of the simple implements on which the city's wealth depended. The wool comb on the right is for carding wool. This is the process by which wool is disentangled and drawn into fibres ready for spinning the thread; however, a denser comb with shorter nails would be

A 'turnshoe' shoe-maker's bench in The Museum of Norwich

needed to produce finer yarn with longer fibres used for worsted. Worsted is a smooth cloth without a nap that was particular to Norwich and the surrounding villages, such as Worstead from which the name derives. The whirligig in the centre is an 'umbrella swift' for winding yarn – either silk or wool. The stand on the left holds two yarn winders on which thread is spooled ready for weaving. The simplicity of these implements emphasises the pre-industrial nature of the early textile business, often conducted in small workshops and attics by family groups.

The final object, at the bottom, sits incongruously amongst tools of the weaving trade. Surely, Woodford wouldn't interrupt his textile cycle by including a different trade? Well, here it is at The Bridewell Museum, a turnshoe maker's bench. Turnshoes are made inside out and then inverted so that the seams are brought inside. It was the leather shoe trade that replaced weaving as the city's number one employer.

Roundel 3C: The Black Death

According to the historian Francis Blomefield the bubonic plague first arrived in Norwich on New Year's Day 1348, but it was to return intermittently over the next three centuries. In the years preceding the first outbreak the city's numbers had been swelled hugely by

The Dance of Death C16, St Andrew's Norwich

Roundel 4A: The Vikings

The Norman legacy of Castle and Cathedral is magnificently tangible but traces of their Scandinavian cousins – the Vikings – are harder to find. They are present, nonetheless, and in this roundel James Woodford acknowledged the significance of the Viking invasion to the development of proto-Norwich. The Great Heathen Army first invaded East Anglia in 865AD but there are few physical signs that Scandinavians settled in Norwich until the tenth century. Then, there is evidence of an Anglo-Scandinavian settlement – a north *wic* on the northern side of the Wensum, centred along modern-day Magdalen Street. It was defended by a looping, 13-foot-deep ditch and probably topped by a bank and fence that may well have been constructed in response to Anglo-Saxon pressure from Edward the Elder of Wessex who overcame the East Anglian Danelaw in 9 I 7. This protected settlement was sufficiently important and stable in the tenth century

the arrival of land-starved peasants coming in from the country to seek work. The Black Death reduced this jam-packed population by about a third to a half and wasn't to return to its original level until the late seventeenth century. Bodies were buried in communal pits in the Cathedral Close and the raised churchyard of St George Tombland; in the Great Plague of 1665-6 Chapelfield was used as a mass grave. High and low were struck down alike as depicted in this Dance of Death from St Andrew's church – the last stained-glass example left in the country.

Nordwic penny ca 930AD.
Courtesy of Classical Numismatic Group, LLC. http://www.cngcoins.com

to have its own mint making Anglo-Saxon 'Nordwic' coins. This example depicts Æthelstan the Anglo-Saxon King of Wessex.

Scandinavian influence can be detected in the naming of churches: St Clement – the patron saint of sailors – was much favoured by the Scandinavians; his churches occur at rivers or portals as here, at St Clement's on the corner of Fye Bridge Street and Colegate. Norwich also had two churches named after St Olave or Olaf, the Norwegian king canonised in 1030.

St Clement's Colegate

The Anglo-Scandinavian settlement was not confined to the northern bank for it extended southwards to form a double burh joined across the river by a wooden causeway where Fye Bridge now stands. A few hundred yards south of the river was the Anglo-Scandinavian marketplace in Tombland, from the Danish word *täm* for open space and it is from their word '*gata*', meaning street, that we have inherited Finkelgate, Fishergate, Pottergate, Colegate, Mountergate etc. What may have caused Nordwic to abscond to the south bank was the raid in 1004 when Sweyn Forkbeard laid waste to Norwich in reprisal for the killing of his sister Gunhilde in the St Brice's Day Massacre when settled

Danes, 'sprouting like cockle amongst the wheat', were exterminated on the order of Æthelred the Unready.

When the French descendants of the Vikings – the Christianised Normans – arrived a few decades later they established their presence on the south side with their cathedral of stone and a castle overlooking a re-sited marketplace where it remains today.

Roundel 4B: Textiles and agriculture

Roundels 3B and 4B. Textiles and Agriculture

On roundel 4B Woodford presents us with much the same layout he used on the facing roundel (3B); they could be mirror images. The wool comb, the yarn winder and the stand in 4B really do reflect the contents of the left-hand roundel; why the repetition? Again, an object at the bottom breaks the weaving sequence but here it is not specifically related to Norwich industry but to Norfolk agriculture. The wheeled plough alludes to Thomas Coke, 1st Earl of Leicester (1754-

The Leicester Monument (1845), Holkham Hall. Courtesy of Sarah Cocke

1842) who, from his Holkham estate on the North Norfolk coast, is credited with sparking the British Agricultural Revolution. He pioneered the harnessing of oxen instead of yoking them and for using wheels on the plough to reduce friction, as a result of which a single ox could draw it through the light Norfolk soil. Perched between the ox and the plough at the foot of the Leicester Monument are English Leicester sheep, an improved breed promoted by Lord Leicester.

Roundel 4C: Kett's Rebellion

Here hangs poor Robert Kett from the walls of Norwich Castle.

The success of the Norwich weaving trade, and the rising price of wool, led rich landlords to enclose common land in order to graze their own sheep. In 1549 Robert Kett, a tanner from Wymondham, sided with those uprooting hedges and fences. Under his leadership the uprising swelled to as many as 15,000 'rebels' encamped on Mousehold Heath. Kett's men defeated forces led by the Marquess of Northampton but were finally overcome at the Battle of Dussindale. Robert Kett was hanged from a gibbet erected on the battlements of the Castle and 'left hanging, in remembrance of his villany, till his body being consumed, at last fell down'. Wymondham Abbey has two towers: one for the monks and one built by the

people and it was from this western tower that Kett's brother William was left hanging by chains.

The eighteenth century historian Francis Blomefield recited the establishment line that Kett's army contained the 'scum of Norwich' but, of course, one man's rebel is another man's freedom fighter and a plaque on the castle walls expresses a more enlightened view that acknowledges the hardship of the times:

'In 1549 AD Robert Kett yeoman farmer of Wymondham was executed by hanging in this castle after the defeat of the Norfolk Rebellion of which he was the leader.

In 1949 AD – four hundred years later – this memorial was placed here by the citizens of Norwich in reparation and honour to a notable and courageous leader in the long struggle of the common people of England to escape from a servile life into the freedom of just conditions'.

Roundel 5A: Chocolate and crackers

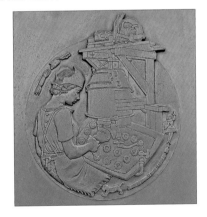

The combination of chocolate-making and Christmas crackers arranged around the perimeter of the roundel could only refer to Caley's for no other confectioner in the city mixed these disparate trades. Twelve years before James Woodford drew this design, Caley's installed 44 chocolate-piping machines so the worker is piping chocolate in their Fleur-de-Lys Factory at Chapelfield.

REPRESENTATION OF TRADE MARK AS ADVERTISED.

CALEY'S

YE SIGN
of ye
FLEUR DE LYS

MANUFACTURED
IN YE OLDE CITIE
of NORWICH,
ENGLAND

Registration of Caley's trade mark 'The Prentices in the Snow' (1899).
Courtesy of Norfolk Record Office.

his sodas were bottled in an old factory in Chapelfield that had made cloth for glove-making but this was just the beginning of Caley's growth. By the 1920s, Caley's factory had expanded, with several multi-storey buildings occupying the block between Chapelfield Gardens and St Stephen's Street.

The crackers illustrated in the roundel date to the late 1880s when Caley's fancy box department expanded into making Christmas crackers. The boxes of this period were beautifully decorated with art nouveau designs by a young Alfred Munnings who had recently trained at the Norwich School of Art. In making crackers, Caley's were competing with Londoner Tom Smith who had invented the snap in Christmas crackers, but in 1953 the two firms merged and traded from a factory once owned by Colman's on Salhouse Road.

To provide year-round employment for his summer workforce, Albert Caley started to make drinking chocolate and in 1886 began to make chocolate confectionery using milk from a farm in nearby Whitlingham. In 1932 Caley's was sold to Mackintosh's, the toffee-makers from Halifax, who modernised the factory and started to manufacture combinations of chocolate and toffee in products like 'Rolo' and 'Quality Street' assortment.

The factory was rebuilt after being badly damaged in the 1942 Baedeker Raids. In 1969 the business was acquired by Rowntree's and then by Nestlé (1988) who sold the site to be redeveloped as Chapelfield shopping mall (2005).

I have a Proustian recollection of the aroma of chocolate that seemed to hang over the city in the 1980s, usually – it seemed – on Sunday mornings. A less ethereal reminder of those days comes in the form of the two granite rollers that once ground the cocoa beans, now used as seats outside the Chapelfield Road entrance to the mall.

By 1883 chemist and druggist Albert Jarman Caley – 'manufacturer of aerated & mineral waters, & ginger ale' – had moved from London Street to the Chapelfield site, presumably to take advantage of a nearby deep well drawing the purest water in the city. Caley lived across the road at The Crescent. As we saw on roundel 2A,

Caley's chocolate factory on Chapel Field Rd, seen in 2003.
© georgeplunkett.co.uk

Roundel 5B: Livestock markets

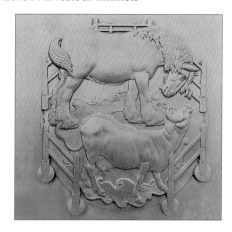

Norwich was the trading centre for a major agricultural county and livestock had been sold at the Castle Ditches or Dykes since at least the time of James II. The 'Market for Horses Cows Sheep & Swine' is clearly marked on Samuel King's eighteenth century map as is the Old Horse Fair, Haymarket, Hog Hill (Orford Hill near the Bell Hotel), Horse Market (now Rampant Horse Street) and the Old Swine Market on All Saints' Green – all contributing to a sense of the city as a hub for the county's agriculture.

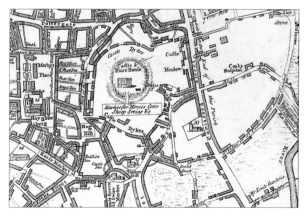

King's map 1766, with markets outlined in red.
Courtesy of Norfolk Museums Service

Stone roller outside Chapelfield Rd entrance to the mall

After the coming of the railways, cattle would be driven from Norwich Thorpe Station to various sites around the castle commemorated in the street names: Cattlemarket Street, Market Avenue, Farmer's Avenue. In 1960 the Cattlemarket was taken out of town to Hall Road.

Roundel 5C: Shoe-making

The City Hall stands on the site of a former Start-rite shoe factory and it is shoe-making that is celebrated in this roundel.

By the 1840s the city's textile trade was in terminal decline and the same pattern of work – production by outworkers controlled by garret-masters – was inherited by the city's rapidly expanding boot and

The former Norvic Shoe Co on Colegate

shoe manufacturing trade. Soon, this piecemeal form of production was overtaken by large-scale manufacture in factories.

Numerous small businesses became consolidated into the Big Five companies that dominated Norwich's boot and shoe trade: Edwards & Holmes; Howlett & White (later the Norvic Shoe Co.); Haldinstein's (later the Bally Shoe Co.); James Southall (later Start-rite); and H. Sexton & Sons (later Sexton, Son & Everard). About the time that Woodford was designing this roundel the Norwich boot and shoe trade was employing about 10,000 workers and the Norvic building on Colegate/ St George's Street was the largest shoe factory in the country. None of the major factories are operating now.

Roundel 6A: Soldering mustard tins

The worker solders tins using a pool of molten lead and a soldering iron, which is shown again in profile on the left. He would have been working on a production line at Colman's of Carrow, famous worldwide for producing mustard. This company's yellow tins of mustard powder were emblematic of the city and it is a great sadness that the factory closed in 2019 after over 150 years at the old Carrow Abbey site.

Roundel 6B: More livestock

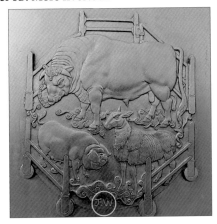

Artist's initials circled

Paired with the 'livestock' roundel on the facing door (5B), this relief shows other animals, including sheep whose fleece was at one time crucial for the weaving industry.

Roundel 6C: Silk weaving

By producing quality worsteds made from combed long-staple wool Norwich became a major centre of the English woollen industry. Trade in this valued export had been affected by the Black Death and was once more diminished by competition from Flanders in the form of New Draperies – mixed, lighter fabrics containing wool mixed with linen or silk. In 1566 the mayor petitioned the Duke of Norfolk to seek the permission of Queen Elizabeth I to invite '30 Douchemen of the Low Countreys of Flaunders' each with up to 10 family members or servants. These Protestant 'Strangers' – whose numbers would soon be swelled by refugees escaping the murderous intolerance of the Catholic Duke of Alba – introduced new techniques and helped the city regain its competitive edge.

Even in the nineteenth century, when the textile trade was in serious decline, silk products, like shawls and 'mourning crape', kept Norwich weaving alive. This roundel almost certainly refers to the firm of Francis Hinde & Hardy who employed several hundred people

Advertising Hinde & Co 1947.
Courtesy of Graces Guide to British Historical Industry.

in St Mary's Works on Oak Street. In the 1920s Hinde's expanded by taking over other Norwich silk weavers; they also built a silk-weaving mill at Mile Cross, owned another silk mill at Oulton Broad, and had showrooms in London.

By experimenting through the 1920s and 30s with nylon and artificial silks, like rayon and viscose, Hinde's seem to have been trying to reduce their reliance on natural silk and so the roundel may well depict the weaving of man-made yarn. During World War Two Hinde's produced parachute fabric. The end of 700 years of textile manufacture in Norwich was signalled in 1964 when Hinde's was bought by the giant Courtauld's who closed the factory in 1982.

The 19th roundel

Norwich's own toothpaste.
Courtesy of Patrick van der Vegt, atlasrepropaperwork.com

According to his designs, Woodford hadn't intended his final roundel to illustrate silk weaving; instead, his original plan had been to show tubes being filled with toothpaste. I did read that the toothpaste was 'Odells' but it turns out to have been 'Odol' by Cranbux Ltd of 103 Westwick Street – a firm owned by Coleman & Co Ltd. Remember Coleman's (with an 'e'), the wine-bottling company represented on the very first roundel (1A)?

We have to ask whether these roundels gave a fair reflection of the city for it's rather puzzling why Woodford even considered the filling of toothpaste tubes when he could have chosen the famous home-grown insurance business, Norwich Union (now Aviva). Woodford's vision was decidedly backward-looking but who in 1936 anticipated the war or could imagine what life would be like in the aftermath of the war, let alone in post-industrial millennial Britain? Amongst many other things, Norwich is now a city of literature and science but it would take a brave person to commission another set of roundels to fix this moment in time.

That was to have been my ending but, serendipitously, I came across someone who *did* have the courage to predict the city's future. In 1935, Walter Watling – founder member of the Norwich Twenty group of artists and Art Master at City of Norwich School in Eaton – drew '*Norwich in AD 2035*'. In his prophetic dream he was introduced to someone over the 'televisophone' who 'promised to send along the glasses and in another minute they arrived by the pneumatic tube delivery service.' He was spot on with his televisophone and Amazon still have time to perfect their pneumatic tube delivery service before the 2035 deadline.

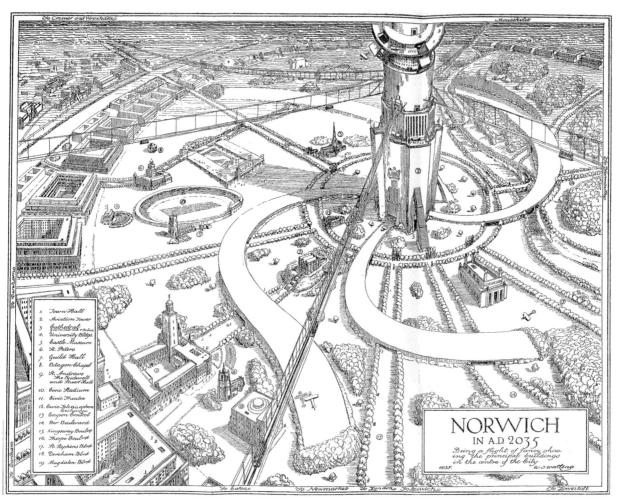

'Norwich in AD 2035' by WT Watling. From 'Snapdragon: The Norwich Hospital Annual 1935'.

ACKNOWLEDGEMENTS

First and foremost I must thank my friend Karen Roseberry for designing the book. This is now the third she has produced with its distinctive square format and all credit for appearance is hers.

I am also grateful to the many who gave their time to provide access to buildings, records and photographs. Special thanks to Jonathan Plunkett for generously allowing free access to his father George's photographic archive of Norwich covering much of the twentieth century; it is an important record and I have leaned heavily on it. Thanks are also due to the magnificent historical services in this county: particularly to Picture Norfolk managed by Clare Everitt; to the staff of the Norfolk Record Office; and to the Heritage Centre at the Millennium Library. David Clarke of the City Bookshop has an enviable library of all things Norfolk and has kindly helped me out on several occasions.

I would also like to express my gratitude to: John and Rachel Allen, Barclay Group Archives, Thomas Barnes of Aviva Archives, Sally Bate, Susan Brown, Sophie Cabot, Pamela Clark, Classical Numismatic Group, L.L.C., Sarah Cocke, James and Matthew Colman, Byron Cooke, Louise Crawley, Geoff Dickinson, John Fielding, Roland Harris, Hill House Antiques and Decorative Arts Ltd, Vivien Humber, Derek James, Caroline Jarrold, Samantha Johns, David King, Bea Leal, Richard Malt, Peter Mann, Stuart McPherson, John Mitchell, My Primitive Methodists website editor, Norfolk Industrial Archaeology Society, Mary Parker, Parson Woodforde Society, Mary Perrott, Cathie Piccolo, Mike Preston, Sue Roe (my patient sounding-board and fellow church crawler), Maria Sienkiewicz, John Snape, Evelyn Simak, Cathy Terry, Kate Thaxton, Alan Theobald, Selwyn Tillett, Philip Tolley, Patrick van der Wegt, Verger St Peter Mancroft, David Vincent, Tom Williamson, Sarah Wilmot, Beverley Woolner, Barbara Worland, Lucy Wrapson.

To all, thank you.